the RETIREMENT INCOME STOR-E!

the RETIREMENT INCOME STOR-E!

*The Story Behind the Launch
of the Retirement Income Store*

DAVID J. SCRANTON

ADVISORS' ACADEMY
PRESS

The Retirement Income Stor-E!
The Story Behind the Launch of the Retirement Income Store

Published by
ADVISOR'S ACADEMY PRESS
Pompano Beach, Florida

ISBN 978-0-9975441-9-0

FIRST EDITION

Book Design by Neuwirth & Associates

Manufactured in the United States

10 9 8 7 6 5 4 3 2 1

DISCLAIMER

David Scranton is an Investment Advisor and Founder of Sound Income Strategies. He is also Founder and President of Advisors' Academy. The information presented by the author and the publisher is for information and educational purposes only. It should not be considered specific investment advice, does not take into consideration your specific situation, and does not intend to make an offer or solicitation for the sale or purchase of any securities or investment strategies. Additionally, no legal or tax advice is being offered. If legal or tax advice is needed, a qualified professional should be engaged. Investments involve risk and are not guaranteed. This book contains information that might be dated and is intended only to educate and entertain. Any links or websites referred to are for informational purposes only. Websites not associated with the author are unaffiliated sources of information and the author takes no responsibility for the accuracy of the information provided by these websites. Be sure to consult with a qualified financial advisor and a tax professional before implementing any strategy discussed herein.

DEDICATION

SINCE 1999, I HAVE been dedicating time to educating my fellow Baby Boomers about the dangers of Wall Street when it comes to their retirement.

This is my third book, my second by a major publisher, and, for the most part, exercising my newfound national "voice" whether in print or on national TV is a job that I really did not want. True, I wanted "someone" to build a national foundation of education and financial solutions; I wanted "someone" to talk about the history of Wall Street to protect those same Baby Boomers from a third and catastrophic drop. Yes, I wanted "someone" to do it, but I sure as heck did not want that person to be me.

I have experts in their field that help me execute my vision, and I truly would not be where I am today without them, but my secret weapon of sorts is about 40 advisors in 20 states who have been with me since the very beginning. They are the closest thing to brothers that an only child such as myself will ever have, and they are who I dedicate this book to, because *The Retirement Income Stor-E* is, as of the writing of this book, as much theirs as it is mine because they said, "If not you, if not us, then who?"

Although not initial franchisees of The Retirement Income Store, the following individuals had an equally material contribution to its development: Doug Ferris, Eddie Ghabour, Jim Lineweaver, Scott McLean, Greg Melia. My original franchisees include: Andrew Agemy, Steve Archer, Mike Burleigh, Jay Carrier, Dee Carter, Tad Cook, Lindsey Cotter, Randy Dorcey, Michael Eastham, Mark Falter, Al Flores, Matthew Johnson, David McAdams, John McCartin, Sam McElroy, Patrick Peason, Drew Pelton, JoAnn Regan, Anthony Sacarro, Jeff Small, David Stearns, Michael Stewart, Russ Stone, Brad Williams, Wes Wood, and David Wright: *Thank you* for making my life's work a source of constant inspiration and learning. Together, we will reach at least 7 out of 10 Baby Boomers, and everyone will one day understand the change from growth to income and how crucial it can be.

The other group I would like to dedicate this book to is . . . the Baby Boomers. Let's show them that we are the first group of Americans who really understand that retirement can be the culmination of a great life, and it should be prepared for with the utmost care and confidence. Make sure you are dealing with an advisor who is a fiduciary and one who understands income.

David Scranton

CONTENTS

the RETIREMENT INCOME STOR-E!

CHAPTER 1

The Income Generation

I F YOU DO A Google[1] search for the word "income," it will generate 974 million results in about 0.62 seconds. And yet, for all the information about income out there, most people still have no idea what it means or how to get it.

I'm talking, of course, about a certain kind of income. Not the kind you receive, as Merriam Webster defines it, in exchange for some form of labor or capital. I'm talking about *retirement* income, the sort of money that comes in the door with little to no "work" on your part, since the whole idea of retirement is to stop working, or at least be able to have the option if you wish.

Investing for income is still a relatively niche field in the financial industry. When you consider the vast number of brokers, financial advisors, and investment firms that specialize in stocks and capital appreciation, and the far fewer who specialize in income, it's like holding up a penny against a dollar bill.

As one of the few financial advisors who have spent the last 20 years focusing on the world of bonds and other income-producing investments, I know why that is, but it still troubles me. At the end of the day, investing for income can be a more conservative way to get a return on your investment. Whether you're investing for capital growth or income, it shouldn't matter as long as YOU are receiving the income you need from your investments. Given the sheer number of folks entering or approaching retirement age today, and the sheer amount of money still allocated to stocks and other risk-on investments, we're standing at the edge of a precipice. If the market decides to take another dive, and I'll explain later on in this book why that's likely, there are millions of Americans who are at or near retirement age who will simply never recover. It won't be like the last two crashes when our generation, the Baby Boomer generation, still had plenty of strong earnings years left in their 40s and 50s to make up for those horrible drops. This time, time is simply not on their side. And with too much of their investment dollars allocated to stocks, it's like playing with fire. Eventually, you're going to get burned.

Unfortunately, most folks who are at or near retirement age haven't received the proper education, nor have the right resources at their disposal, to invest their dollars the right way. In the world of zero percent interest rates, they haven't been told or shown how to invest their money in the abundance of safer, risk-averse, income-producing investments available to them. That's why I've set up a national initiative, The Retirement Income Store, to make these sorts of investments available to anyone who wants them. Because the fact of the matter is, millions of Americans need these types of investments available to them since they're safer and they have less exposure to the ebbs and flows of the stock market. But sadly, the average financial advisor has no idea where to look or how to find them.

MORE INCOME, LESS RISK

I've watched the world take some pretty crazy turns during my career as a financial advisor. From the financial mania of the 1990s to the two meltdowns[2] in the 2000s, I've seen peaks of maximum greed and bottoms of peak fear. What troubles me the most as an advisor with thousands of clients I've served over the years is that there's still a great deal of confusion about how people who are at or near retirement need to approach allocating their life savings.

On some level, I think most people understand they're supposed to de-risk as they age. Does that mean switching to a 60-40 bond/stock portfolio where the majority, 60 percent, is in bonds and other income-producing investments, with the rest is still in stocks? Does it mean settling for low-yielding Treasury bonds that pay 2, maybe 3 percent? Most people who are at or near retirement, the types of people who need to be making these sorts of decisions, have no idea. As I'll discuss later on in this book, most advisors don't either.

Most people who are approaching retirement today were brought up in the glorious days of the 1980s and 1990s bull market when the stock market grew more than 10 times its size. The Dow soared from 776 in 1982 to 11,772 at its peak in the year 2000. At that time, Baby Boomers, or what I like to call "The Income Generation" who were born during the years between 1946 and 1964, were between the ages of 36 and 54. Some were approaching retirement age, but most were still firmly in their earnings years where retirement was still a long ways off. Even the oldest members of the Income Generation still had 11 years before they started retiring at age 65. There was time to recover.

So while a 50 percent market crash between 2000 and 2003 hurt badly, it wasn't the end of the world. But then the unthinkable happened. The market recovered into 2007, only to crash by another 58 percent into 2009.

I suppose I don't have to remind you how painful this was, but most people whose careers began in that glorious bull market of the '80s and '90s had no idea this sort of thing was even possible. The financial industry as a whole had come to believe that average annual returns of 15 percent were the new norm. And yet, after nearly 20 years of gargantuan growth, it wasn't until the year 2013 that the stock market finally achieved a new high.

Chart A

That's 13 long years of zero-net growth.

By this point, the "young" members of the Income Generation[3] were now between the ages of 49 and 67. Many were now entering retirement age while the rest were approaching it. Today, that range is 55 to 73.

We're now firmly in retirement territory.

Only this time, it will be much, much more difficult to recover from another 50 or 60 percent crash if it hits.

Fortunately, there's a better way. You can reallocate your investment dollars to the world of bonds and other bond-like investments to continue generating a steady income stream. The only difference is, you're investing for income, not growth. I'll explain the difference a bit later.

YOU CAN'T TIME THE MARKET, BUT . . .

There are lots of people out there who like to say it's impossible to time the market, which is really just an idea Wall Street likes to sell to convince you to constantly leave your money in stocks. If you're constantly pulling your money in and out of the market, you might miss the bad years, but you might miss the good years, too. That's why the conventional wisdom that you can't time the market is true, but only to a point.

I made a major switch in my career back in 1999: I switched from a stock-focused model to an income-focused one. I knew that average annual returns of 15 percent weren't sustainable, so I pulled most of my clients' money out of the market near the top. To be sure, I was met with a little resistance, but as the market started to crash in 2000, my clients quickly realized I was onto something.

A similar thing happened in October 2007, when I warned my clients in our monthly newsletter that another crash was likely, and that this time the Federal Reserve[4] would likely try new, untested tactics to stop the market from crashing to an absolute low. While I didn't know it at the time, the market quite literally peaked that month, and sure enough, quantitative easing and zero percent interest rates became the theme over the next decade.

With that kind of track record, some might call me a visionary, even psychic. I'm not. What I am, fundamentally, is a math guy. In fact, mathematics was my major in college. I told my guidance counselor that I wanted whatever field of study where I'd never have to write a paper. Funny now that I'm writing my third book!

But I am also a student of history. From my study of over 200 years of stock market cycles, I understand that the possibility of a third and fatal crash is not only possible, but likely. And you don't need to be a math guy to understand that Baby Boomers aged 55 to 73 can't afford another crash if their life savings is tied up in the stock market.

I hate talking about it, because I'm right there with you, and aging is a scary thing. The more we age, the less time we have. It affects our minds and our bodies, but also our finances.

Unfortunately, as we've learned all too well this century, the market can crash at any moment when the majority of folks least expect it, robbing us of half our money and, even worse, robbing our time. The older we get, the less time we have to recover from a market crash if we still want to retire.

If you're already retired, and you have your money exposed to the whims of the stock market, you're even more at risk.

Unfortunately, this is the situation that most of today's retirees find themselves in and it's just one of many hurdles they face on their path to enjoying a comfortable retirement.

That's why I have a different name for our generation. I don't call us the Baby Boomers. I call us "The Income Generation." Because we need a paradigm shift so we can start thinking about this situation differently.

We don't need stocks. We don't need risk. We need income.

THE UNTOLD TRUTH ABOUT RETIREMENT

In 1941, *LIFE* magazine[5] was the first to note the emergence of a growing "baby boom," as older couples who might otherwise have had children during the Great Depression at long last felt financially prepared to make the plunge into child-rearing.

However, we didn't define our generation until nearly a quarter century later, when, in 1963, newspapers began warning of a tidal wave of college enrollment as the first "Baby Boomers" were reaching college admissions age.

It's time we start thinking about our generation a bit differently.

We're way past college and many of us are winding down our careers. That's why I have a different name for our generation due to the financial challenges we face as this massive wave of 76 million people marches deeper and deeper into its retirement years.

We are "The Income Generation" for one simple reason—our generation needs retirement income, because it's a safer, more consistent way to get investment return. Unfortunately, most of our generation isn't getting it yet.

It's not hard to understand why this is the case. The idea of retirement is a relatively new one. It's not that people only recently decided they didn't want to work all their lives. It's that people are just living longer.

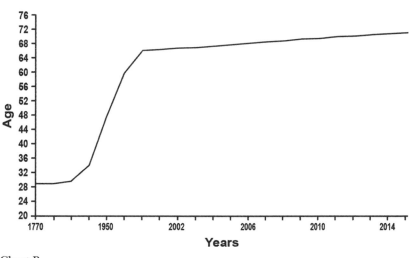

Chart B

In the Middle Ages, people were lucky to reach the age of 40. After the Industrial Revolution,[6] human life spans took off. And over the past century, lifes pans have essentially doubled.

The idea of retirement, while it dates back to the late 18th century, didn't start popping up until the late 19th and early 20th centuries, or just over 100 years ago.

Anytime you hear the phrase "there are only two kinds of people in the world," it's usually the start of a bad joke. However, for thousands of years, that truly was the case. Prior to the mid-19th century, we had the haves and the have-nots. There was no middle class to speak of. There was no one who needed to "retire." The idea hadn't been invented yet!

That all changed with the Industrial Revolution. With the expansion of industry and our economy, we began to see the birth of a third kind—the middle class, which has come to define all the hallmarks of the modern era, namely democracy, innovation, and capitalism.

It's important to put these sorts of things into perspective because they are a big reason why we're facing the issues we are today. It hasn't been that long in the course of human history that we've had extended life spans, a middle class, and all these other trademarks of modernity that have made the idea of retirement not only necessary, but possible. So, it should be no surprise that, as a society, we're still figuring out what retirement really means, and, more importantly, how one should go about it.

Here, in short, is why I'm writing this book: Members of the "Income Generation" need income because it's a safer way of getting return. They need assurance that they won't lose their life savings should another market crash start to unfold, and they need a consistent stream of income coming in every year so they can retire without having to withdraw from their life savings or having to go back to work.

Until now, there have been very limited avenues for members of the Income Generation to get this much-needed income. Most financial advisors are still stuck in the '80s and '90s mindset where stocks were, and to them still are, the only game in town. More importantly, investing for income requires a kind of experience that most advisors simply don't have. It's not as simple as investing in Treasury bonds or buying a CD. It's a matter of wading into the pool of corporate bonds, preferred stock, and other income-generating investments that most advisors don't specialize in.

WHY A RETIREMENT INCOME "STORE"?

So, why am I calling it a "Retirement Income Store"? Because I believe investing for income should be as easy as walking into a department store, buying what you need, and calling it a day.

Department stores, after all, are one of the greatest symbols of the middle class and the consumer economy.

When Macy's[7] opened its first department store in New York's shopping district in 1858, it was especially clear that we had sailed into uncharted waters. The middle class had taken control, and their shopping needs demanded change. For the first time in history, people had a one-stop shop that satisfied all their needs: clothes, furniture, bedding, appliances, and on and on. You name it, Macy's and other department stores such as Hudson's and Marshall Field's[8] provided it. It was the clearest example of the driving force of the middle class. No longer did the elite determine the course of the economy behind closed doors, but society was now catering to the needs of the much larger middle, and nowhere was that more evident than in the department store.

Today, department stores aren't what they used to be, thanks to discount retailers and, more recently, to the e-commerce boom via online retail giants such as Amazon. But there's no discounting the fact that the department store has been a staple of American life for every generation of the last 150 years. And I think there's some beauty to the idea that you can go to one place and find everything you need.

That's exactly what today's Income Generation needs—not for consumer goods, but for income.

YOUR ONE-STOP, SHOP

My career began with the idea of a "one-stop shop," a "financial" department store, if you will.

I started out at a small, independent financial firm in Hartford, Connecticut, in 1987 that sought to meet every need of a person's financial life in our small town. Our primary focus was life insurance, but as the firm expanded, we branched out into other areas. Eventually we hired a CFA who took control of our clients' investments. We brought on an estate planning attorney to handle our clients' estates. We even took on an accountant to help our clients out with their finances and taxes.

This isn't a revolutionary idea today, but 30 years ago, it was ahead of its time. Back then, everything was separate. You had brokers in one office, insurance agents in another down the street, and accountants and tax specialists somewhere else. What my firm did is take all of those separate branches and put them together, a one-stop shop that local citizens could come to, in order to meet all of their financial needs.

I didn't think about it back then, but that one-stop shop over 30 years ago really set the tone for the rest of my career and a mission that I hope will shape the financial life of every American for the better.

Today, we need a different approach when it comes to investing. The traditional "stock market model" no longer works. It's been broken for the better part of the last 20 years, ever since the tech bust that wiped out half the market cap of the U.S. stock market. And yet the majority of the American investor population is still stuck in the same mindset of the 1980s and 1990s when it seemed as if stocks could only go higher.

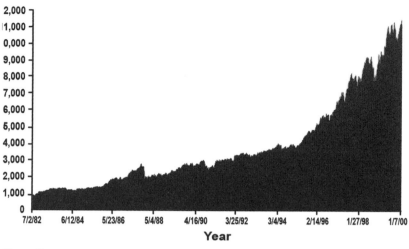

Chart C

Stocks truly were the only game in town back then, or at least the only game that mattered. The Dow closed July 2, 1982, at 797. By January 7, 2000, it had reached 11,522, growing 14 times its size, a gain of 1,346 percent. After that kind of financial mania, it's no wonder why folks look back to the "good ol' days," wishing for annual rates of return of 15 percent, double the market's long-term average.

But I don't plan to just write another hackneyed financial planning book that tells you how the old way of investing stinks and why investors need to better reposition themselves for retirement. I'm actually doing something about it.

For years I have been working to establish a national network of financial advisors that can help the more than 76 million Baby Boomers face the challenges of investing in this new era of heightened volatility and risks in the market, what I call The Age of Economic Uncertainty.

Fact is, of the more than 200,000 financial advisors at work in the United States, the vast majority of them are not equipped with the proper tools, knowledge, and resources to guide their clients to financial security in this era of increased uncertainty. Most of them were brought up in the '80s and '90s, the longest secular bull market on record, when stocks were all you needed to get rich. They were not trained to understand the challenges that investors and retirees face when stocks *do not* go up for many years. Those challenges only get harder the closer you get to retirement age. So, for many years, I've been working hard to spread this message and bring more people into the fold.

But, in the last couple of years, I've had to face a harsh reality.

I realized that I could never hope to take on the financial establishment, and the years of faulty thinking that lies therein, without taking my mission public and building it out on a national scale.

That's why I launched "The Retirement Income Store,"[9] a one-stop shop that any American can access to quickly reposition themselves for retirement.

To my knowledge, no one has assumed the mantle to carry this message to the American people, at least not on this large a scale. The idea of investing for "income" has grown in popularity over the last several years, as more and more investors have said "phooey" to the market's schizophrenic whipsaws. It is still very much a niche approach to investing. The old stock market model still prevails, and unless retirees or near-retirees reposition themselves soon, before another catastrophic downturn wipes them out for good, they may never be able to enjoy the retirement they've worked their entire lives to deserve.

That's why I've decided to take my message directly to the American people themselves, to you. If financial advisors won't make the leap on their own, my hope is that enough people will demand a change that financial advisors will have no choice but to create a sustainable investment portfolio for their clients.

THE DEFINITION OF INSANITY

I believe Albert Einstein[10] is quoted as saying "the definition of insanity is doing the same thing over and over again and expecting different results." That standard approach to investing, the stock market model, worked for most of the 20-year period spanning the 1980s and 1990s. But it's been the complete opposite during the last 20 years of the 2000s and 2010s. Investors have been hit by not one, but two major 50 percent drops, and while the market seems to climb ever higher in the face of economic uncertainty, we are still haunted by the ghosts of 2000 and 2008.

Yet the vast majority of the American investing population is still stuck in the same mindset that hasn't worked for the last 20 years, simply because it worked in the 20 years before that.

It isn't their fault. Fact of the matter is, financial advisors were never taught how to invest their clients' money during long-term secular bear markets, and they're so beholden to Wall Street's interests that they have little choice in the matter. For them, it's always a matter of what pays the mortgage and what puts food on the family table. I'm sure we can all relate.

However, it doesn't change the fact that the old way of doing things no longer works.

The more you age, the more difficult it gets to financially recover from another 50 percent drop that wipes out half your savings. If you're at or near retirement age, the question no longer becomes how much you need "saved up" in order to retire; it is how much money you can generate from your savings without having to risk your money in the stock market.

In other words, how much *income* do you need?

I understand this probably isn't the first time you've heard this, but how many times have you heard this without someone offering a clear, written-out solution?

There hasn't been a national initiative in place to help protect the countless men and women who are at or near retirement age today that will, most likely, be wiped out if the market takes another nosedive. The way you do that is by helping people invest their money for income, since it's a safer, more conservative way to get return.

The national initiative is my mission; through advertising and awareness campaigns, we are illustrating how the average consumer can set a goal for retirement and have an income specialist (who is also a fiduciary) help them set a solid plan all based on income, not hoping and praying for growth in the stock market.

I'M NO PERMABEAR, BUT . . .

I want to get one thing straight: I'm not a bull on the stock market. And I'm not what you'd call a "permabear" either.

There are some people who have been calling for another market crash since 2011, back when the most recent bull market was just getting its legs.

So while I'm no stock market cheerleader, I'm no "doomsayer," either.

What I am is a man in his 50s who understands, plain as day, that if I get hit by another 50 percent drop in the stock market, which is a historical certainty, as I'll prove in the subsequent chapters of this book, my financial life will never be the same.

More importantly, I'm a financial advisor who understands that very same truth applies to my clients.

If a drop of that magnitude occurs and we haven't taken the right precautions, the fact is you and I will likely not be able to enjoy the same lifestyle in retirement that we plan on enjoying today.

Let me put my life in some context for you.

To be clear, I have money. But I'm far from what you would consider "rich."

I grew up in the small town of Bristol, Connecticut.[11] Nowadays when everyone hears that, their first thought is ESPN because that's where their headquarters is. I grew up way before ESPN was established. Even today, it's still a small town of some 60,000 people, so you can imagine what it was like growing up there in the '60s and '70s.

My parents didn't come from money. They were hardworking, middle-class folks like I'm sure your parents were. My dad worked construction, and my mom did factory work. As their son, I decided it was my prerogative to create a better life for myself than my parents had so I could one day offer a better life to my children in turn. That's why I went into the financial industry. I wanted to learn how money worked. I wanted to learn how to make enough of it that I could work on my terms and someday retire, on my terms.

I've done very well for myself, but I'm by no means "rich." I don't own a huge yacht or some $10 million McMansion, but I do own two very nice waterfront homes, one in Florida and one in Old Saybrook, Connecticut, and I don't like to skimp on dinner. I've worked hard to enjoy the life I have and I plan to continue.

I sat down before I started writing this book, and I asked myself, "Dave, how much money do you *really* need to retire?" Now most people think $5 million sounds like a whole lot of money. Yet, if you withdraw the standard 4 percent per year, you are talking about a gross income of $200,000 per year. And, if I gross 200K before tax, it's going to net about 144K after taxes (assuming a 28 percent tax bracket). That's not too bad. But now, let's look at my expenses. My property taxes on both properties amount to about 50,000, my utilities are 24,000 a year, and my average Visa bill is about 5K a month. So, if you add those figures up: 50K on property taxes, 24K on utilities, and 60K on Visa, that's 134,000, leaving me only 10,000 for everything else, including medical insurance.

So the point is, I would be forced to change my lifestyle and either skimp on those dinners going forward or I would have to sell one of my homes. I would have to make adjustments even looking at a $5 million retirement.

Now to be clear, I may be overexaggerating certain line items such as property taxes and utilities; I like to be overprepared. But to have literally no spending money from a $5 million retirement shows you how serious this situation is. There is a gap here that might mean 4 percent might not be enough, it might force me to eat into that principal. At that rate, I'd run out of money after a couple of decades if the stock market doesn't keep going up, so I better hope and pray I don't age very well into my 70s and 80s. That's also assuming I don't face a major medical emergency that sets me back tens, if not hundreds of thousands of dollars in a single year, which, with the way medical costs are skyrocketing, seems entirely likely.

My point is, even if you have a $10 million nest egg, you really have to *plan* if you want to retire. You have to dot every *I* and cross every *T*. The reality is, most Americans won't have anywhere near that much when it comes time to retire. Most folks, who will actually be able to retire, may only have $250,000 or $500,000 in assets. Others might have $1 million or $2 million. Unfortunately, retiring will not be easy for any of them if, and this is a big if, they stick to the same strategies Wall Street has been shoving down their throats for years.

STOCKS WON'T BUY YOUR RETIREMENT

If you have your money in stocks, you know stocks are anything but consistent. One year they're flat. Another year they're up 20 percent. Another year they're down 50 percent. Every year seems to bring something different.

So let me ask you, do you want your retirement to be subject to the whims of the market's chaos? Are you prepared to make sacrifices on a year when the market's down? Will you have the discipline to take some of your cards off the table when the market's up?

If you don't want to have to work that hard and you want to save yourself the headache, you need to be prepared to do something different.

You see, there's another reason why the 4 percent rule (which is explained later in the book more fully) doesn't work. The 4 percent rule assumes that in order to retire, you need to have reached a lump sum. It assumes a specific dollar threshold you need to have met before you can stop punching the clock.

If the goal of retirement is to enjoy it, let me ask you this: Does the idea of withdrawing from a lump sum, hoping it will grow back and watching it disappear year after year, sound like fun to you?

Do you like the idea of starting with $1 million in assets and, partway through your retirement spending it down to $500,000, hoping that last half of a million will last you the rest of your years?

That kind of thinking doesn't appeal to me, nor does it to anyone else for that matter.

When I make money, I like to keep it. Chances are, so do you.

That's why retirement isn't about a lump sum. It's about income.

There's a reason we don't spend our savings in our younger years. It's because we want the money to be there later in case we really need it. So why do we think it's okay to spend our savings after we've retired?

Is it because we know we could be dead in a few years?

If so, isn't that kind of morbid?

I have an alternative solution.

If the goal of our working years is to build up a certain-sized portfolio of money, then the goal of our retirement years should be to never let it shrink.

You might wonder how that's possible. If the goal of retirement is to quit working, don't the funds for our expenses have to come from somewhere?

They do, but they don't have to come out of your principle,

your lump sum, your nest egg, your net worth. They don't have to come out of stocks you sell year after year.

It can come solely from the income you generate from your investment.

THE ONLY THING THAT MATTERS

What I'm about to tell you might sound crazy; it doesn't matter how big your nest egg is.

The only time it will ever matter is when it comes time to have a bragging match with your neighbor about whose personal assets are bigger, and who cares?

Think about it like this.

If you budget your money, you don't think about the money you have sitting in savings, because the whole point about saving is not to touch it. Instead, you think about the money you have coming in the door each month. You think about your income. You think about the income you need to pay those bills. If we go through life knowing we're not supposed to spend our savings, why should that change at age 65 when we know we might have a solid 25 years left? That's why you can't afford to spend down the money you've worked so hard to save over the years. You need that money to stay around as long as possible so you can continue to collect income by investing that money in carefully selected fixed-income investments.

When you spend down your principle, your money only works for you once. But when you can collect *income* off it, it works for you year after year after year.

That's why the only thing that matters if you're at or near retirement age is NOT how much money you've accumulated, how many stocks you have, or anything like that. It's how much *income* you can generate off the wealth you've acquired.

In the following chapters of this book, I'm going to reveal, in precise detail, why income is the ONLY thing you need to concern yourself with at this stage if you are anywhere close to retirement.

I'm going to show you why the average financial advisor is not equipped to help you protect your life savings or safely invest your money. I'm also going to show you the steps you can take to find someone in your area who specializes in generating income for retirement and what you can do if there isn't someone near you.

I'll tell you why our economy hasn't been the same for the last 20 years and why it lends itself to the kind of 50 percent and 60 percent drops we've suffered.

Most importantly, I'll show you why another crash is not only likely, but a historical guarantee if one is looking at history as your primary guide.

Finally, I'll tell you about the work I'm doing to start a grass-roots revolution that sweeps the financial landscape, bringing a Retirement Income Store to every American who realizes that, in the face of economic uncertainty, a conservative, income-based approach to investing is the only way to go forward.

I promise this won't be like every other financial planning book you've read that only offers platitudes and half-baked solutions. If I've done my job, this book will change your life, and for the better.

Strap in. It's going to be a wild ride.

CHAPTER 2

So What's the Big Deal About Income, Anyway?

If I were to ask you what the difference is between a 16-year-old and a 60-year-old, you might tell me, "Everything." To be sure, there's no one correct answer. The way I see it, the biggest difference that comes with age is the way we set our goals.

At 16, the sky is the limit. Our bodies are powerful, vibrant, and full of energy. We believe we will someday write the next great American novel, discover a cure for an incurable disease, or become an Olympic gold medalist.

Said another way, we're all over the place.

Before life teaches us its hard lessons, it's impossible to determine what is really the most important thing to us. When we're young, we have grandiose ideas of taking on the world and pursuing our passions. But we have no specifics. Early in life, our dreams are so amorphous and abstract because we don't know what we really want. As we age, our goals become more focused.

After decades of work, all we wish is to be able to fulfill purpose-based goals that are important to us, retire someday, make sure we will never run out of money, keep up with inflation, and, for some, to leave a modest legacy. Sometimes, our purpose become even more modest—having family at our side, food on the table, and our finances secure.

It's not about settling. It's a matter of setting more focused goals based on where you are in life. Your investment strategy should obviously follow suit. It should have a specific and defined purpose.

And smart investors are, indeed, purpose-based investors.

PURPOSE VERSUS PERFORMANCE

Purpose-based investors are those who invest with an end goal in mind. To buy a new car, renovate a home, leave financial worries behind, or retire and leave the world of hard work behind.

Some, however, are what I refer to as performance-based investors. These are people who are so competitive they strive to get the maximum return possible with almost no regard to their goals and purpose or risk, as if investing were some type of contact sport. It is almost as if maximizing return on investment gives one some sort of bragging rights.

Imagine holding your investment statement up to the neighbor's window to proclaim, "Ha ha, I made more money than you last month." Sounds silly, right? But that's essentially what performance-based investors are all about.

Men in particular tend to be more susceptible to this. It's in our DNA. For countless years, our biological history has programmed us to fight for power. If we're not strong, someone else will come along to overpower us, take our land, our women, and our wealth. We're addicted to our own search for power because power is what makes us survive.

This survival mechanism can misfire, just as our own search for power can sometimes blind us.

That's exactly why so many folks are drawn to the stock market.

Yes, the uphill climb of the stock market is exciting. When you buy a stock and it goes up, you feel like a genius. When it goes the opposite way, you feel defeated, and that can affect more than just your finances.

- Stress
- Depression
- Decreased libido
- Higher blood pressure

That's what's so tricky about stocks. Anyone can promise they've found some three-step formula for identifying the market's biggest winners. The fact of the matter is, investing in stocks is hard. There's no sure thing when it comes to it. Stocks can rise 20 percent one year and fall 50 percent the next.

Here's the thing. Life shouldn't be about working *harder* to obtain power, wealth, and security; it's about working smarter to obtain these things. It's not about being the "best." It's about wisdom and strategic thinking, purpose versus performance.

The Bible says God awarded Solomon for being wise. Solomon was by many accounts the richest man in human history. There's something to take from that.

MAXIMUM RETURN, WHAT FOR?

If performance-based individuals are completely honest with me when we first meet and discuss their investment goals, they would tell me their goal is to get maximum return with minimum risk.

That's a good start. But it's only a start. It's like saying "I want to be happy" without any clear idea as to what happiness really looks like, or what it takes to get there.

The problem with this, as self-actualized individuals realize, is that money is represented by green pieces of paper with pictures of dead presidents. In other words, money itself does not lead to happiness; it is how we eventually *use* that money that brings joy, fulfillment, and a sense of purpose to our lives.

The question that I have for performance-based investors—retired or approaching retirement—is, "Maximum return for what eventual use?"

The way I see it, money can only be used in three ways:

1. **An eventual lump-sum purchase:** A second home, yacht, a luxury vehicle, etc.
2. **Retirement income:** Money coming in the door so you can stop working.
3. **A legacy for others:** Money left over after you die so your family doesn't have to work as hard.

So allow me to ask you, which of the above represents your *primary* purpose with a majority of your retirement?

The fact is, most people don't really need a second home, a yacht, or a new fancy car. Most people don't feel compelled to leave any significant or lasting legacy in terms of passing on money to future generations. In fact, leaving too much money to your children or grandchildren can create problems for them later in life.

However, everyone *needs* retirement income to last them until the day they die, unless they plan on working forever.

If you answer this question by choosing number two, you would be in agreement with the vast majority of clients I've sat across from and asked this very question to.

Of course, I'm not staring at you from across a desk asking you to be "real" with me. In your head, you might have answered number one or number three. That's okay if you did. There's no need to be shy; it's just you and me here.

The fact is, some of my clients answered differently. For those who answered something other than number two, I usually ask them what they would do in the following situation . . .

Let's say you retired from my company and I've got $1 million set aside for you as a retirement benefit and you have two options how you could take it. Option A is to receive our company stock. Of course, you can't sell it right away because you're an employee; it's restricted stock. But you can collect a 2 percent dividend on it, each and every year. That's $20,000 in income. That's Option A.

Option B is the old type of defined benefit pension plan where I simply pay you $60,000 a year for the rest of your life. You don't get any stock, but no matter what, you get $60,000 a year for the rest of your life. That is your pension.

Which option do you take?

I realize it's hard to turn down $1 million, but you have to realize something. Until you can sell that stock, that money isn't really yours. It's restricted. You can't even list it as an asset on your balance sheet if you go to the bank and get a loan.

Sure, you get $20,000 in income. But in some respects, that's the best you'll get with Option A. Essentially, the 1 million lump sum is unusable because if you were to spend it, you'd lose your income. Only the 20K per year income is usable. With Option B, you get $60,000 a year no matter what. The key to how people make this decision is that, in the first scenario, only 20K is usable. With Option B, the entire 60K is usable, year after year . . . big difference.

I present each of my clients with this scenario, and each time, without fail, they say they'd take Option B for $60,000.

This teaches us something valuable. When you are planning for retirement, it really is about income, isn't it? Which would you choose?

ABOUT THAT "PENSION," DAVE . . .

Of course, most pensions are a thing of the past. If you were to retire from your job today and an employer offered Option A for

$1 million in restricted stock with a 2 percent dividend or Option B for $60,000 in income for life, you'd be lucky to get either option. This isn't the sort of thing companies really do anymore.

In the post-war era, as industry was expanding, companies had a shortage of workers, and they used pensions as an incentive to bring new workers aboard. Today, the situation is much different. Good jobs are more competitive, and most companies simply aren't as desperate.

So, although retirement is all about income, you don't need me to tell you that traditional pensions and Social Security aren't what they used to be.

TRADITIONAL PENSION PLANS

The first retirement program popped up in 1889 when the chancellor of Germany, Otto Von Leopold, Prince of Bismarck,[12] announced that workers who attained the age of 70 would be provided a pension annuity, financed equally by workers and employers, and underwritten by the government. And while the United States started experimenting with pension programs in the late 1880s, it wasn't until the Great Depression that the idea of a "social safety net" became popularized. It remained popular until the 1980s when interest rates in general started to decline. Because of this, employers had to make bigger and bigger deposits into the pension to fund liabilities. That, plus the increasing popularity of mutual funds, gave employers a chance to pass that liability on to employees through self-funded plans such as 401(k)s. Today, if you have traditional pension benefits, consider yourself lucky.

SOCIAL SECURITY

The Social Security Administration was signed into law in 1935. As a sort of funny story, the first person to receive Social Security benefits actually lived to be 100 years old. Ida May Fuller[13] paid into the Social Security system for 3 years and received 35 years' worth of benefits. But she was an anomaly. Back then, if people even lived to be 65, they might only collect Social Security for a couple of years so they could wind down their affairs before they quickly passed away.

Today, people are living well into their 80s or 90s, but we still retire at the age of 65. As a result, Social Security benefits proportionally aren't what they used to be and many feel like they will not be able to count on them.

The challenge presented by traditional income vehicles like pensions and Social Security is what makes the Retirement Income Store today so important.

We can't rely on these vehicles the way that we used to. And since there are no sure things with stocks, they're not a reliable option for retirees, either.

That's why, today, the question is no longer how much money you've saved up; it's not about how big your "number" is, and it's not about performance. The question now is: How much *income* can the money you've saved up make you, even as it continues to grow?

ANSWER THIS QUESTION

Let me ask you an important question: How does the amount of money you have in the bank, or in the market, affect your day-to-day life?

Really think about your answer to this.

If you're reading this book, there's a 99 percent chance you have a modest amount stowed away in a savings or 401(k) plan. There's also a decent chance you rarely or never touch that money, so it's money you're not supposed to spend. It's called "savings" for a reason.

So, besides a lingering thought in the back of your head, the amount of money you're "worth" doesn't affect your day-to-day life much, does it?

After all, the money we have stowed away isn't the money we typically spend. We use income for that. What money do you use to pay your bills? Put food on the table? Fund hobbies? Pay for travel? Buy gifts for grandchildren?

It's not the money you've accumulated over the years; whether it is in stocks, bonds, or stacked away in a savings account.

It's your *income*. And that doesn't change in retirement.

Unless you want to spend down the money you've accumulated over the years in retirement, and leave yourself in a situation where you have less money producing less income, this situation applies to you.

So let's get one thing straight: The amount of wealth you have is only as good as the amount of *income* it can produce when you enter retirement.

Again, I understand that, for performance-based investors, what I'm saying requires a bit of a paradigm shift. It requires a different style of thinking than they've been taught after years and years of growth-based investing.

During our working years, it makes sense to grow our money so we have plenty of income to draw from in retirement.

But as we approach retirement, continuing to grow our money and subjecting ourselves to the risks that come with it is the wrong approach. It's about using the money you've accumulated by a certain point to produce enough income to afford yourself a nice retirement.

RETIRING COSTS MONEY

There's another reason why income is so important in retirement. It's expensive.

You adopt a new hobby. You start traveling. You might go out to eat a bit more. And while all these things might keep you young and active, they cost money. Heck, even if your hobby is reading, you still have to spend money to buy books.

Ask yourself, what is your retirement dream? Do you want to have a purpose-based retirement where your life continues to have meaning for yourself and others?

Hopefully, the whole point about retirement is finally giving you a break. It's giving yourself an opportunity to be a young adult again without responsibilities or worries and living life on your terms.

But you need income for it.

Retirement's just plain expensive. It's a luxury, and luxuries cost money. You have to think about it in those terms.

Most people I work with tend to underestimate just how expensive retirement will really be. The problem is that when you stop working, you not only have less income coming in the door, you have a whole lot more time on your hands. And unless you plan on sitting at home watching TV every day of your retirement, you're going to need income in order to fill that time with activities that enrich your life.

A U.S. Bureau of Labor Statistics[14] news release in 2017 shows that the average American 15 years and over watches 2.77 hours of television each day. The average retiree, meanwhile, watches 4.37 hours per day. I can almost assure you those retirees aren't following our business model, because if they did, they wouldn't be sitting at home all day. They'd have the income they need to enjoy their retirement the way they're meant to.

As stated above, your expenses tend to go up when you retire.

Start getting used to that idea now, because if you accept it early on, you can be better prepared when the time comes.

It's not something to be ashamed of, either.

You don't have to go into retirement with a humble frame of mind thinking you have to count your pennies.

If you're the type of person who is reading this book, chances are you were the type to cut expenses along the way. You were a good steward of your money. When it came time to buy a new car, and you had the option to buy an expensive car or a more afford- able one, you probably chose the more affordable one because it was cheaper and more practical. You probably took conservative vacations. You probably picked the less expensive house.

The point is, you worked hard for the money you have now. You saved it by making practical decisions along the way.

Why skimp on it now?

If you made sacrifices along the way to get where you are now, don't you want to *enjoy* yourself in retirement?

So, let's get two things straight about retirement:

1. It's more expensive than you probably think it is.
2. It isn't worth skimping over. If you worked hard to save your money, you have a duty to yourself to enjoy it.

I've had a lot of people walk into my office who make $120,000 a year and try to convince me they'll only need $3,500 a month in retirement. I ask them, "Are you banking the extra 70 grand each year?" That's when they start to realize they'll probably need more than $3,500.

Bottom line, you don't retire to skimp and save. You retire to enjoy it. To do that, you need a plan. More specifically, *you need income.*

STAYING SEVEN MOVES AHEAD

So, you know you need income. Through most of your life, you had to sit in an office or show up to work eight hours a day, five times a week in order to earn it. The trick of retirement is to keep that income coming in the door without having to work for it. Easier said than done, right? It's also to keep that income coming in on a consistent basis so you never have to spend the money you worked so hard to save up, unless you choose to (see "lump-sum purchase").[15]

The way you do that is simple in theory, but, as you'll discover in this book, a little more difficult to execute. That's because most financial advisors don't have the right plan.

To set up an ironclad retirement income plan, you need to be able to work with an advisor who can put you in income generating investments and who understands that your expenses will most likely increase as you age through your retirement years.

Inflation is one of the big reasons why. It is the hypertension of retirement, the silent killer. You have to remember that every year your expenses will typically rise by 2 to 3 percent. That means you have to have enough coming in the door to offset that. If you're using the traditional retirement income model, where you withdraw from your principal every year and have less and less money generating less and less income, it's like being attacked from both sides. Less money coming in the door plus higher expenses is a recipe for disaster.

Most people have a hard time accounting for inflation when they think about retirement. That's because most people, figuratively speaking, are flying at 1,000 feet. At that altitude, you can only see so far ahead, less than 40 miles, in fact.

My job as a financial advisor is to take a 30,000-foot view. At that altitude, one can see over 200 miles, five to six times as far. It is where I can see the rest of a client's life ahead of him and plan it out for him each step of the way.

The average investor can only visualize their life maybe 5 or 10 years ahead, and that's simply not far enough. It is said that the average chess player can only think one or two moves ahead whereas the grandmaster can think seven moves ahead. It takes a lot of practice games to become a grandmaster. Trouble is, investors only have one shot at retirement.

That's why finding the right advisor is so important.

With inflation rising at 2 or 3 percent every year, think of it like this—in 30 years, the dollars you've saved up today may only carry you a third as far as they do today. That means your investment income doesn't just need to be able to meet your living expenses today, it needs to be able to do it 30 years from now.

AHHH, HEALTHCARE

Inflation is just one of many concerns, and a good financial advisor will factor this into the equation, making sure the income you have coming in the door will account for it.

The biggest concern for retirees that almost always makes retirement more expensive than they ever could have imagined is healthcare.

I have an aunt and uncle who passed away not too long ago. By many standards, they were rich. They retired in their early 50s, had homes in different parts of the country, including one in Hawaii, went on cruises a couple times a year, and lived a really good lifestyle.

When my uncle finally died in his 90s, he was within six months of running out of money.

Why?

Well, it wasn't because they overspent during their healthy years, but because their full-time in-home healthcare had been running them about $150,000 to $200,000 per year *for years*. As bad as it was for them, for us, it will be even worse.

Healthcare costs are subject to some of the greatest inflation rates in the country. The only other things that come close are college tuition and childcare. In the last 18 years, inflation has grown at an average annual rate of 2.2 percent.[16] Since 1948, the price of medical care has grown at an average annual rate of 5.3 percent compared to 3.5 percent for the consumer price index overall.[17] So, at close to six percent, healthcare and medical costs are essentially doubling every 12 years. That means if a couple in their 60s is budgeting $200K for annual full-time in-home health care today, by the time they're in their late 80s or early 90s, those expenses could be four times as high—as much as $800K a year. And, even if they're projecting an increase based on the standard inflation rate of 3.5 percent, they're still going to fall short.

So, today, if you have $2 million in an IRA, you could afford to have nurses run around and take care of you full-time for 10 years. But if your investment allocation is not optimal for generating income, you won't have the full $2 million. Starting at age 70 and a half, the government is going to make you start taking those pesky required minimum distributions (RMDs), leaving less money left over for later. So, by the time you need in-home health care, your IRA balance may be down to $600,000. Combined with healthcare inflation, those 10 years you could have afforded today are suddenly down to one or two years by the time you need it the most.

If you've ever had a family member in a nursing home before, I'm probably correct in assuming one of your goals is to never end up in one of those places.

I say, if you can't use your money to keep your independence, then what can you use it for? That's a big reason why you want to keep your money for later years when you might actually need it.

Until then, you need to keep your principal intact. You need to use the money you've accumulated to generate income to cover your expenses and to cover forced distributions for as long as possible, knowing somewhere down the line, you might need to tap into your dear old nest egg.

PLAYING THE LONG GAME

Inflation and healthcare are no doubt two of the biggest concerns retirees face, and two of the biggest reasons why a modern retirement plan needs to position your portfolio toward *income* instead of *growth*. But there's another side to it.

A lot of retirees make the mistake in thinking they don't need income from their investments because they have some coming in from a pension and Social Security. When you take a 30,000-foot view and look at the expenses you could be facing 20 to 30 years out, you realize you can't afford for your investments to dwindle because of an involuntary withdrawal such as RMDs.

Here's why: Most retirement sources such as traditional pensions simply don't have an inflation hedge or a cost of living adjustment. It doesn't matter how much your living expenses change due to inflation. These retirement vehicles will pay the same dollar amount regardless.

Social Security *claims* to have an inflation hedge, but it doesn't. Not really. One of the biggest scams with Social Security is that, after giving you a cost of living adjustment, they increase the cost of Medicare part B[18] accordingly. The problem with that is, Medicare part B premiums come out of the Social Security benefit.

Essentially, they write you a check with one hand and take it back with the other. But most people who aren't retired don't know that.

So, you might have some money coming in the door from a pension, if you have it, and Social Security. That's fine, but you need additional income to make up for the fact that these sources don't have an inflation hedge.

Think of your investments as a truck with a towing hitch. No longer does the truck have to pull only itself, it now has to pull itself and the tractor or broken-down vehicle it's towing. If you expect to collect a pension and Social Security, those payouts won't go up just because inflation does.

What this means is that the income you collect from your fixed-income investments is doing double duty, it's not just towing itself, but it has to pick up the slack from these other investments that don't have an inflation hedge built in.

This is why you can't afford to spend the money you've saved up over the years. The income you collect on this money already has to work hard enough picking up the slack from these other income streams that don't have an inflation hedge, and if you spend down your principal you'll make it that much harder.

LEGACY

So, if you're a purpose-based investor, and your primary goal is to generate retirement income now or in the near future, here are reasons you need to focus on investing for income instead of leaving yourself subject to the whims of the stock market.

Number one: You worked hard for the money you've saved and you should be able to spend it on your terms. Retirement is something to be enjoyed, and the way you do that is by having your money work for you.

Number two: Inflation means you need to have enough income to keep up with rising prices.

Number three: Healthcare—you can't spend your money down now because you'll need it more at a later time.

That leaves number four, which is legacy.

Many people are motivated by the mere fact that they live in a country where we have the ability to transfer money at our impending death to those that we love and care about. For many of us, that is a very personal decision. And it really doesn't matter what or whom you wish to leave a legacy to. It's only important that you protect your money to the extent that it goes to that person or entity that you designated in your will. Not the government and not Wall Street.

The reality is that you didn't work hard all your life just so you could give all your money back to Wall Street because you're using cancerous financial strategies, taking forced distributions from principal, or you got caught up in another fiscal meltdown. You made these sacrifices for a reason. So whether you want to set up a trust fund for your children, give your money to charity, donate to your church, or whatever philanthropic cause you choose, your money can make a difference in someone's life and many will remember and thank you for it.

It really just boils down to this: Do you want to have as much money by the time you're 80 as you do now, or less? If you stick with Wall Street's model, I can almost guarantee you'll have less. If you invest for income, and withdraw those mandatory distributions from the money your fixed-income investments are generating, instead of from your principal, you have a good shot of keeping your money intact well into your golden years when you need it most.

It all depends on what you want in life.

When we were young, we all had big dreams and lofty goals. Then we got a job. Then we got married. Bought a house. Had a child. Had another child. Suddenly, you had a mortgage to pay and four children you had to send off to college possibly all on one income.

After all that, retirement sounds pretty good. Forget the lofty dreams and goals. If done right, retirement can be more than a dream; it can also be a lot of fun.

But to do it right, you need a plan.

OFFENSE AND DEFENSE

There are two phases of the retirement planning process. The first is the accumulation phase when you scramble to make as much money as possible so you can someday retire. The second is the income phase when you're planning gets more strategic. Call it the difference between offense and defense.

In the accumulation phase, you're investing for growth. You're heavily invested in stocks, pouring money into your 401(k). Since you have time on your side, you're less concerned about the market taking a dive because you know it will allow you to buy more stocks on the cheap and make up for it later. Ninety percent of your investment advisors are perfect for this.

However, once we get into our 50s, we become a little bit more concerned about those potential market crashes. By this point, we've built up a sizeable nest egg. Retirement is a spitting distance away. Yes, we could always use more money, but we also realize we're betting with time.

WELCOME TO THE INCOME GENERATION

That's when we begin our switch to investing for income. In the income phase, we're going defensive.

It's the time of our life when we can't afford to lose our money. Sure, retirement may only be 5 or 10 years away. That leaves several years left to accumulate money; this is done mostly during our highest earnings years. We can already start to feel "it." Our bodies are already starting to wind down. We're not as young as we used to be, as our doctors painfully remind us.

Retirement is coming.

Eventually, work gets tiresome. We want to slow down. We crave a simpler life. By that point, we have to use the resources available to us to continue to survive.

Social security isn't going to cut it, and the pension system, if you even have a pension, is in terminal velocity.

We simply can't rely on entitlements to fund our retirement for us.

That's why we're left with two choices, WITHDRAW money and hope we never run out, or develop a plan that generates INCOME and makes it almost certain that you'll never run out, and never have to worry about running out, either.

CHAPTER 3

A Retiree's Best Friend

THE IDEA OF RETIREMENT is a relatively new one in the course of human history. So it should come as no surprise that we're still working out the kinks. We need to bear that in mind as we approach the idea of it. There are no hard and fast rules when it comes to retirement. Most of the conventional wisdom is based on a short blip in human history.

That's one reason why retirement planning is so hard.

Because the idea is still so new relative to human history, only a small part of the population is successful in achieving what one might consider a "comfortable" retirement. I'm talking about one where you have little or no drop in income between your last day of work and your first day of retirement, cost of living increases all the way, and little or no chance of running out of money.

The thing is, a lot more people are capable of enjoying a comfortable retirement if they adjust their mindset.

For many years, retirement professionals considered the "4

percent rule"[19] to be the magic number for retirement planning. That is to say, starting at the age of 65, you can withdraw 4 percent of your principal once a year and rest easy knowing you'll probably never run out of money. So, according to this "rule," if a retiree has $1 million, he or she can withdraw $40,000 each year "safely," essentially engineering income through these withdrawals.

But it gets trickier the more we age. The government says that, starting at age 70 and a half, you have to start taking mandatory distributions from your IRA[20] and 401(k). Those distributions start at 3.65 percent. By your mid 70s, they're up over 4 percent, and by your late 70s, they're over 5 percent.

So, automatically, the 4 percent rule doesn't work. By the time you reach your late 70s you have to withdraw more, and if you aren't generating income from your investments, you have to withdraw it from your principal.

However, if you could stick with it, the 4 percent rule was considered "safe" through a mathematical model called the "Monte Carlo Analysis."[21] This is a process that examines the universe of historical outcomes over a long period (such as 30 years) based on certain parameters. It produces a weighted-average probability of success. For this exercise, success is traditionally defined as the probability of not running out of money during that 30-year period. So, if one has $1 or more remaining 30 years later, it is considered a successful outcome.

Some investment companies have actually created marketing pieces using the "Monte Carlo Analysis" touting the results of their "moderate risk" portfolios. These are portfolios that are only partially exposed to stocks, between 60 percent stock and 40 percent bond or vice versa. These results have assumed a 4 percent withdrawal over 30 years and shown an outcome of greater than, get this, an 80 percent chance of success, as if that's a good thing.

In other words, following their model, you have an 80 percent chance of your money living as long as you do. Which means there's a 20 percent chance that your money doesn't.

So tell me, if I were the greatest salesman in the world, could I ever convince you to turn your life savings over to me if there were almost a 20 percent chance of running out of money?

Or, think of it this way. In a game of Russian roulette,[22] there's typically only one bullet in a six-bullet chamber. That means you have a 16.67 percent chance of losing your life; you also have an 83.33 percent chance of survival.

So it's pretty close to the 80-20 scenario above.

Truth be told, those aren't *bad* odds. They're actually quite good. If four people make it out and only one person has to bite the bullet, it's certainly not the worst imaginable scenario if you are one of the four people who make it. But it's not funny anymore if you turn out being contestant number five.

THE RIGHT WAY TO CASH OUT YOUR MONEY

When it comes to life and money, the potential reward of a moneymaking effort is only as good as the potential risk.

Unfortunately, a lot of investors today are playing Russian roulette with their money.

But it gets worse.

Most Monte Carlo analyses use stock market performance and interest rate assumptions going back many, many decades. This of course, in theory, encompasses good times and bad times alike and therefore is not attempting to be predictive in any way. The stock market returns over the last two decades have now begun to water down the long-term averages as lower interest rates have now done for the bond markets (lower rates that many believe are the new normal). More recent studies from reputable sources have published results of similar Monte Carlo analyses showing that a 2.8 percent withdrawal rate over 30 years in a 60/40 or 40/60 portfolio yields a 90 percent chance of success. In other words, an investor with $1 million can now "safely" withdraw only $28,000 a year. And there is still a 10 percent chance of running out of money.

That's why the only way to safely spend money in retirement is to take it from the interest and dividends you collect, not from your principal.

The average person who retires today is expected to live 20 to 30 years into their retirement. If you start chipping away at your principal too early, you leave yourself vulnerable in later years when you have less and less money upon which to draw interest.

Think of it like a 30-year mortgage. Each month our mortgage payments are fixed. That way we know what we're spending each and every month and we can prepare for it financially. But the breakdown of each payment changes the longer we pay it off. At the beginning of our mortgage payments, we mostly pay interest. That's because, each month, we pay 1/12th the interest on the remainder of the mortgage we haven't paid off. If you have a $300,000 mortgage at 4 percent interest, and your fixed payment is $1,100 a month, $1,000 of that first payment goes toward paying interest and only $100 pays down the principal. The next month, your interest payment drops to $999.67 and you pay $100.33 in principal. Eventually, you chip away at it long enough that your fixed payments mostly go toward principal and not interest.

Retirement works the same way, but in reverse.

Imagine paying a mortgage is like slowly filling a hole, whereas your principal in retirement is a pile of money that, as you chip away at it, produces less and less interest, forcing you to take more and more away each month. One month you might only take $100. The next you take $100.33. It starts small, but the problem progressively worsens and, after 30 years, you're out of money.

If you're lucky, maybe you won't live that long, but I find it a little morbid and counterproductive to plan and hope for an early grave.

DOLLAR COST AVERAGING . . . IN REVERSE

If you are invested in the stock market or in mutual funds, it gets worse. Remember when you first started contributing to an IRA or 401(k) and someone told you that you were doing a great thing because you were dollar cost averaging? By contributing a constant amount of money into mutual funds each pay period, you were able to actually buy more shares when the market was down, essentially lowering your average purchase price.

Let's assume that you were contributing $100 each pay period into a fund. For the first pay period, the average fund price was $10 per share so you purchased 10 shares. For the second pay period, the unthinkable happened and the fund dropped to $5 per share and you made your deposit anyway.

The question is: "What was your average cost per share after two pay periods?" If you said $7.50, you are in the vast majority of people whom I query. But the correct answer is $6.66 per share. This is because you bought twice as many shares when the fund price was cheaper and half as many when the fund price was more expensive. Dollar cost averaging[23] helped you "buy low," which of course is the first half of what successful investors always try to do, "buy low and sell high." That's why market corrections can actually be a good thing, when we're younger and we have more time on our hands. It gives us an opportunity to buy assets on the cheap.

It's different when you're retired because you are no longer a net-contributor to the market, but instead, a net-distributor. When you have money in stocks or stock funds and the market drops, your money still has to come from somewhere.

The problem, though, is that the math works exactly the same as above, but in reverse. That puts you in a situation where you have to SELL more shares of stocks or mutual funds when the market drops, just the opposite of what successful investors strive to do.

That's called "reverse dollar cost averaging,"[24] and it's one of the most dangerous strategies there is.

When you're reverse dollar cost averaging, your money depletes even faster than in that 30-year mortgage example above. You end up in a position where you cannibalize your portfolio and leave less of your assets available to draw from later on. Life is filled with zero-sum-game examples where things work great in one direction but not in the other.

It's like trying to put toothpaste back in a tube. It's easy enough to get the toothpaste out, you just squeeze, but if you've ever squeezed too hard and too much comes out, it's a little harder to try to put the toothpaste back in. This is where strategic planning comes in.

THE MOST IMPORTANT EQUATION IN RETIREMENT PLANNING

Commit this equation to memory:

$$\text{Total Return} = \text{Income} + \text{Growth}$$
$$\text{T.R.} = \text{I} + \text{G}$$

Where Income is represented by interest or dividends,
and Growth by capital appreciation.

Let's say that you have $1 million at retirement and that you need $40,000 each year from this sum in order to retire. In essence you are utilizing the withdrawal method and adhering to the 4 percent rule. Also, let's assume that your portfolio is yielding a 2 percent dividend; that means $20,000 a year is coming from the "I." That also means that you will have to achieve at least 2 percent growth or generate $20,000 from the "G" each and every year to be able to get the cash flow you need. Now make no bones about it—you are still taking principal, selling shares on a regular basis. It's just that you're hoping that it'll grow back each year.

Now, I am sure that you don't need me to tell you that, over a 20– or 30–year retirement, you will not generate $20,000 in growth each and every year. Some years, the growth will actually turn into a loss. In fact, you can count on it probably two or three times, out of every 10 years.

I'm a pilot. Part of getting my license was knowing each emergency procedure backwards and forwards. I'm expected to have plans A, B, C, and D for virtually anything that can go wrong while I'm in the cockpit.

So, what's your backup plan?

What will you do in the years when your investments fail to generate $20,000 from the "G"?

1. Are you willing to go back to work?
2. Are you willing to live on less income and sacrifice your retirement goals?
3. Are you going to risk drawing from your principal, knowing what you know now? Knowing you could run out of money?

Do you really want to have to think about this and put yourself in that situation?

THE INCOME METHOD

The good news is that you don't have to. The alternative, a far more secure method, is to invest for the "I," not the "G." If you could generate your $40,000 from interest and dividends (and you can), then your principal can stay intact. All of a sudden it doesn't matter if your investments drop in value, as long as the income does not change. No more worrying about plan B or C.

By keeping your principal intact, you increase your options later in life. If you reach your 80s and feel as though inflation is having a greater impact than originally anticipated, perhaps then you can begin drawing down principal. Or, if you find yourself needing in-home healthcare, you might be really grateful that your principal is still there.

As my good friend Patrick Peason[25] says, "If you want retirement to be stress free, invest for the 'I' and not the 'G.'"

I'd rather take all my money from the "I" and leave my principal fully intact for future inflation, medical payments, leaving a legacy to my loved ones, and, most importantly, having peace of mind that I'll never run out of money in retirement. The American Institute of CPAs[26] conducted a survey and found that 57 percent of financial advisors reported that their clients' top fear was running out of money in retirement. A similar survey asked workers over the age of 50 to rank their tops fears, and 60 percent reported being more concerned about running out of money than they were about death.

In other words, we fear *financial* death more than we fear physical death. Again, it goes back to our earliest paradigm. We made a lot of money in the '80s and '90s. For the last two decades, we've fought to hold onto it. Now we're terrified to lose it.

However, there's a better way. You don't have to leave your money in the market, constantly fretting about another 40 percent drop or worse.

You can invest for the "I" and ensure you never run out of money and that you're worst fear never becomes a reality.

INVEST LIKE YOU'RE RICH . . . FOR INCOME

It should come as no surprise, but retirement is a lot easier if you have deep pockets.

If you have $5 million and only need $100,000 per year from the "I" to cover your goals, that's just 2 percent. You might just be able to keep a good portion of your invested money in the stock market. If we incur another major correction, you won't be forced to sell anything at a loss as long as companies don't cut their dividends.

The problem is that most people with that kind of money live a good lifestyle and simply don't wish to live on $100,000. The good news for them is that, at this asset level, they have access to companies or advisors that specialize in the world of the "I." Now they may not invest for the income quite the way we do, but they do a decent job.

This brings us to the real problem. Most average investors, those who really need retirement income, don't have $5 million. They historically haven't had enough assets to access the proper expertise necessary for income investing. That's what the Retirement Income Store is meant to fix. I'm in the business of helping people make what they have work. Many of my clients have less than $1 million, some far less, and between that and Social Security, we're able to fund their retirement without ever having to draw from their principal.

TEST YOURSELF: WHAT WOULD YOU DO IN THIS SCENARIO?

Imagine you own a 30-unit apartment building and you want that building to be the basis of your retirement. You have two choices. First, you could convert it into condos and sell off one unit each and every year to generate cash flow; and, second, you could rent the units and live off the income.

If you convert it to condos and sell one off each year, you are essentially hoping that the value of each unit appreciates annually to kind of, sort of, replace the value of the unit sold last year.

This may seem to be a good plan for a few years, but as the number of remaining units dwindles, you may find yourself experiencing stress and anxiety. Why? Because after 29 years, you will only have one unit left and that unit has to sell for enough money to last you the rest of your life.

It's not just about waking up after 30 years and suddenly realizing that you've run out of money; it's about the painful process that occurs between now and then. Ten years into retirement, you start to realize that you only have 20 units left but you are in almost as good of shape physically as you were 10 years ago. The prospect of living more than 30 years seems to be more of a possibility. So you start to cut corners financially. Perhaps you take fewer vacations or decide to keep the old jalopy on the road for a few years longer. You find yourself making excuses to your friends as to why you can't go to dinner or to your grandchildren as to why you can't travel to see them more often. You analyze and agonize over every dollar spent. Now, you have been retired for 20 years and are still pretty healthy. But you only have 10 units left. So you begin to stress even more as the cycle spirals out of control. It's enough to drive someone crazy, and make no mistake, it does. I've known people, like my uncle, who amassed great fortunes in life and by the time they died were out of money. It's not a position you want to put yourself in.

That's where the second option comes in: renting all 30 apartment units and living off the rental income. No excuses to friends or grandchildren and no telling your spouse that he or she can't buy something. You can spend each year's rental income with a clear conscience knowing that there will be more next year. Remember when your children were little and too sick to go to gym class? You had to give them a permission slip. Think of this as a permission slip from your advisor to spend 100 percent of this year's rental income and this is where it gets to be fun.

A short while ago, I stumbled upon the Barrett-Jackson auto auctions. I was shocked to see how reasonable some of the prices were to buy mint-condition muscle cars from the '60s and '70s, the very same muscle cars that many of my male clients wanted back then but couldn't afford to buy.

Most people later in life wouldn't spend the money on a luxury like that even if they could afford it. Why? Because they are programmed to think that they have to purchase it from principal, and, after all, once you spend principal, it's gone forever. Many of my clients who are investing for the "I" are not spending all of their income. I couldn't help but think that, with their excess, many could own that car of their dreams without ever spending a dime of their principal. Without having to touch principal, it's a lot easier to get a permission slip from your advisor, or your wife for that matter, to buy that muscle car. Or from your husband to do that kitchen renovation you've been talking about.

As my good friend Greg Melia says, "Don't eat the chickens, eat the eggs. That way you will always have more eggs."

If you want an ongoing supply of eggs, you need to think of them as usable and the chicken unusable. Retirement just requires a slight change of thinking if your primary purpose-based goal is income now or later. The income you generate from your principal is your usable wealth. Your principal—the money you actually use to generate your income—is your unusable wealth. That's the money you can't touch; otherwise you create a slippery slope for yourself where every year you have to draw more and more from your principal until eventually you run out of money.

Our corporate airplane carries 301 gallons of fuel—292 gallons are usable and 9 are unusable (in the fuel supply lines, etc.). At the end of the day, which one really matters? Do you care how much money you have sitting in principal, knowing you can't spend it? Or do you care about how much money you have coming in the door, your income, the money you actually get to spend?

If you can acknowledge that you'd rather have $60,000 a year in usable wealth rather than $1 million in unusable wealth, it should be an easy decision to make.

If you're not trying to make a big lump-sum purchase, and you're not trying to leave a big legacy, there's only one thing left to do with your money if you're at or near retirement age—invest for income. Go for the "I." We're past the accumulation phase of our lives. It's time to enter the income phase.

And here's the thing: This isn't some newfangled idea. All I'm talking about is getting back to the basics.

This is how our parents used to invest their money back in the 1940s, '50s, '60s, and '70s. Back before we had 401k(s), a multitrillion-dollar stock market, and an addiction to mutual funds, our parents invested their money conservatively and wisely in reliable companies that paid a stable dividend, and in bonds and other bond-like investments that paid an above-average yield. It wasn't until the later part of the past century when we all collectively lost our minds in the financial insanity of the greatest bull market on record.

Now, it's time to sober up.

I can assure you, this stuff isn't rocket science. But to do it right, you need to work with someone who specializes in it. You need someone who specializes in investing for the income; I'm not your typical stock market guy.

CHAPTER 4

Don't Fall for This Trap

INVESTING IN THE STOCK market is, at its core, a zero-sum game. A stock is bought by an investor who thinks it will go up and it is sold by an investor who thinks it will perform poorly. In the end, for every winner, there will be a loser. It's the same with gambling, and, similar to gambling, in the investment markets its Wall Street's casino, where the house always wins.

In the case of the stock market, the average investor is constantly fighting a losing battle against the big institutional players. The "house" I am referring to is the business that initially received new capital during the public offering as well as the companies (underwriters and such) that assisted in the public offering. That is the "social good" of the stock market, allowing companies to raise capital so they can afford to employ individuals or buy capital equipment from companies that can employ more individuals in return.

The reality, though, is that most stock market investors never participate at all in this function of the market; that is, they participate only in the speculation of whether that stock price will rise or drop after that social good has already been accomplished. For every seller that thinks its price will drop, there is a buyer who thinks it will go up; only one will be correct. Even among the sharpest minds on Wall Street, if you are correct 55 percent of the time, you are doing well, but even then, the house has already won.

When we're young, we can afford to gamble. We have money to lose. More importantly, we have time to lose. But with each passing year, time is increasingly not on our side.

I don't know you. I don't know your exact financial situation. My guess is that, if you're reading this book, you're either at or near retirement age. You're the kind of person who's at an age where it's time to consider reducing their risk in the stock market and switching to an income model like the one I've been advocating since 1999.

While I may not know your exact situation, one thing I've learned after working with clients for the past 30-plus years that is true for everybody is this—nobody above the age of 50 is financially prepared to lose half their money.

Of course, nobody *wants* to lose half their money at any stage in life. In our 20s, we probably didn't have a lot of money to begin with. The same was true, to a lesser extent, in our 30s and 40s as we began accumulating wealth. But after 50, it's no contest. Why? Because simple math says that if you lose 50 percent, you have to then earn 100 percent just to break even. Think about it: If a dollar drops to 50 cents, that 50 cents, has to double to get back to a dollar. Doubling represents a 100 percent gain. During the two times this has occurred since the turn of the century, it has taken 7 and 6 years, respectively, and no one says that next time it couldn't take 10 years. If you lose half your money after age 50, it's very hard to bounce back. It's nearly impossible.

The truth is that there's only so much your money can grow between ages 50 and 60. For most, best case means it might double. If you happen to catch a tailwind in the stock market, it makes it that much easier.

But how much are you willing to leave to chance?

What if I told you that it's possible to continue growing your money without subjecting it to the risks that come with investing in stocks?

I realize this is a big paradigm shift for a lot of people. We've grown up thinking stocks are the only game in town.

Mutual funds, particularly stock mutual funds, are still one of the most popular investments in America because they hail back to most investors' earliest paradigm. We think back to the '80s and '90s when mutual funds were all the rage and did quite well for the average investor.

It's been a very different story for the last 20 years. Since the year 2000, most mutual funds haven't even matched the market. Many of them even lose money in years when the market is going up. In fact, a recent study showed that between 2002 and 2017, 92.2 percent of large-cap funds lagged behind a simple S&P 500 index fund[27]. Said another way—less than 1 out of 10 professional money managers beat the market consistently. That same study found that 83.05 percent of these funds actually lag behind the market, meaning more than 8 out of every 10 money managers fail to match their benchmarks. And yet, most investors are okay owning mutual funds because they remember how great they were over 20 years ago.

Make no mistake, it is an addiction. We've been conditioned to think that growth is the only way to get return, that "G" is the only way to get "R."

We've all had dreams of becoming the masters of our financial destinies, even as we lay beholden to Uncle Sam and Wall Street and so many other forces that work against us.

What I'm saying is that you can still get reasonable returns by focusing on income investments in this market environment without having to play Wall Street's game.

But it requires a paradigm shift.

YOU'RE NOT WARREN BUFFETT

There are three things you need to understand if you're going to "invest" in stocks. 1) You're gambling. 2) You are overpaying for stocks. 3) The stock market has tidal cycles, and it's hard to swim against the current.

Number one is going to be an unpopular point, but it's worth mentioning.

If you own stocks, I want you to stop thinking of yourself as an "investor." You're not. Technically, you're a speculator.

So what's the difference?

An investor is someone who puts his money into a business with a *plan* for making it pay off. A speculator is just along for the ride.

If your plan is to buy shares in stocks that go up, I'll tell you right now, that's not really a plan. It's a wish.

We were brought up to think that if you put your money in the market, it's an investment. And yes, there's a *chance* it will pay off. But that doesn't make it an investment. I could go to FanDuel[28] and bet on the New England Patriots and make money. Sure, I won, but that doesn't mean I invested. I gambled. "Speculation" is just a fancy market term for gambling with one's money to make it sound less like you're throwing it away.

So, if you invest ANY money in stocks, you have to remember one simple truth: Unless you are purchasing a controlling stake in the company that gives you a seat at the table when it comes time for that company to make decisions about the future of its business, you are not actually investing your money. You are speculating.

Warren Buffett is an owner of businesses. He buys controlling stakes in companies. He *invests* in them in every sense of the word. Us? We're just buying a minority interest and speculating on the board of directors and that the management team in place is going to do a good job.

So, unless you're Warren Buffett,[29] you're not an investor. You're a speculator. You're betting in Wall Street's casino, and remember, the cards are always stacked in their favor. The house has already won.

Let's say that I did go to FanDuel and bet on the New England Patriots. Some people might say, "Well, Robert Kraft and I, our goals are aligned. If the team wins, we both make money." And they might be right up until that point. However there's a big difference. Robert Kraft[30] as a business owner can decide on who the coach is going to be. He can decide whether he's going to play Brady or not. He can decide if he is going to renew Gronkowski's contract, because he's a player who gets injured all the time. He can make these decisions, but the guy betting on FanDuel can't. So, although the goals might be aligned, the guy betting on FanDuel is a pure speculator, whereas Robert Kraft is a business owner.

So now, take that metaphor and compare it to the average investor versus Warren Buffett. "Well, I'm going to follow Warren Buffett as a stock picker since he's good at picking stocks." Not exactly, because he's not a stock picker. He's an owner of companies, and he's a really good owner of companies.

I've worked with a lot of retail investors over the years. Every single one of them believes that they will not lose when they speculate their money. Every person thinks they have some edge, some secret that will help them get ahead. They've thought of something "no one else has" that almost guarantees they'll make money.

And every one of them is shocked when it doesn't go their way.

That's why it is important to understand this. If you put any money in the market, you are speculating. Not investing. That's okay up to a certain age. If you have a job and intend to work for several years, if not decades, you know you have income (there's that word again) coming in the door. That income buys you time so that if you lose any money today, you can always make it back in the future. The equation completely changes when you approach retirement age. Suddenly, you don't have money to lose. You don't have several years of income left to buy you time to recoup any losses you might suffer today.

So, if you put any money in the market, it can only be money that you can afford to lose.

Listen, I get it. Putting money in the market is fun. It's fun like gambling is fun. But gambling is also addicting, like drugs or alcohol, and it's not good for you. That's why, if you are approaching retirement age, and you put any money in the market, you must remember this—you are essentially gambling and potentially throwing your money away.

Yes, perhaps you'll make money, or perhaps you won't lose all of it. But that is the mentality that you must have once you reach the age where you do not have money to lose.

Maybe it won't hurt for you to put a small amount of capital, say $200, into a highly speculative, small-cap stock that could potentially rise hundreds or even thousands of percentage points. Then again, maybe it will. Do you have $200 to lose?

HOW YOU'RE OVERPAYING FOR STOCKS

I won't win any brownie points here either; all stock market and mutual fund buyers are overpaying for stocks and they have no clue.

Imagine that you and I are buying a business together that is selling for $10 million. I am buying 51 percent and you are buying 49 percent. The question I have for you is, "How much should each of us pay?" If you said that I should pay $5.1 million and you pay $4.9 million, then I want you as my business partner.

Typically, the majority owner, with controlling interest, has to pay a premium for that control; the minority owner gets a discount for lack of control. A typical arm's-length negotiation would end up with me paying $6 to 7 million and you paying $3 to 4 million. I am paying almost double for control.

Now apply this same logic to the stock market. Doesn't it make sense that a majority shareholder should have to pay more to control the company, and that minority shareholders should get a discount since their money doesn't get them a seat at the table?

Why is it then that when one publicly traded company issues a tender offer to buy a controlling interest in another company, the premium they typically offer to have a successful outcome is only 10 or 20 percent? Not 100 percent? So, consider the two possibilities here. One, is that the board of directors of the acquired company is giving the acquiring company a below market deal. The other, and the more likely, is that we, as minority share investors are overpaying for our minority interest shares every single day that the market is open.

This is one of those things that Wall Street doesn't want you to really think about, because once minority interest investors come to realize they're overpaying for shares, and losing more money than they should when the market tanks, they'll be up in arms.

In many ways it's a ponzi scheme. As long as there are new "investors" coming in, the scheme can continue to show returns. And as long as our stock market addiction continues, those prices can continue to hover and levitate.

So, as a buyer of stocks, it's important to remember that the cards are stacked against you. Its Wall Street's house, and the house always . . . you get the picture.

That brings us to the third point or problem about investing in the stock market: tidal cycles, or as I like to call them, "market biorhythms."

MARKET BIORHYTHMS

Have you ever asked your broker how long is the "long run"? If you haven't, then allow me to answer that question for you. First, I need to ask you a question.

Do you believe, generally speaking, that history repeats itself more often than not?

Personally, I do believe that history repeats itself, especially when it comes to the stock market.

You've probably heard, read, or been told that the stock market traditionally delivers about 9 to 10 percent average returns over the long, long term. That "average" is actually the sum of two "averages." Over time, 6 to 7 percent of that long-term average comes from price appreciation; the remainder, 2 to 3 percent, comes from dividends.[31]

9 to 10 percent Total Return =
6 to 7 percent Growth + 2 to 3 percent Dividends

However, those averages can be misleading. It doesn't mean you'll get 9 to 10 percent every year. Some years you'll make a lot more, some years a lot less. And some years you'll lose money.

Think of it this way. Suppose two friends claim they are jogging buddies. They tell you that they average 15 miles a week. But, upon examining their exercise routine, you discover the real story. One of them is an exercise nut, who runs 30 miles a week, and the other is a couch potato who prefers watching professional football. Technically, they still average 15 miles a week between the two of them, but the details paint a very different picture of real performance.

The real story of the stock market is exactly the same.

History tells us that the 6 to 7 percent long-term growth rate[32] actually comes in clumps. There are long periods of time where the market moves up and down and in the end experiences zero growth, absolutely nothing, zilch, nada, and long periods where the market averages 10 to 15 percent growth. To use Wall Street's lingo, there were times when the stock market slept like a bear and then ran like a bull. Let me demonstrate by showing you the last 100 years.

Average 0 to 10 percent Growth	Average 10 to 15 percent Growth
1899–1921	1921–1929
1929–1954	1954–1966
1966–1982	1982–2000
2000–	???

Table A

As you can see in Table A above, the actual periods on the left were periods of flat net performance. That doesn't mean, for example, that during the 1899 to 1921 period the stock market declined for 22 years straight. There were good years and there were bad years, but history is very clear here. The good years and bad years washed each other out, resulting in zero net growth for 22 years.

It's also worth noting that the second greatest bull market of the last century occurred just before the Great Depression, and the greatest one just before the tech bubble.

THE LONGER VIEW

Now, if by some chance you're a statistical nut like me, you may wonder what stock market cycles looked like before 1900. The answer is that they were about the same. We consistently had 20 years or so of bear markets followed by shorter bull markets followed by 20 years or so of bear markets.

Together, history suggests these bull-bear cycles tend to last approximately 35 years. Statistically, that means the stock market should outperform all other asset classes over a 35-year period.

If you can survive for 35 years without having to pull any of your money out of the market, and you're comfortable sitting through long periods of net inactivity where stocks swing wildly from one direction to the next, you might as well leave it in. If you can't, you should explore other options.

BEWARE THE TOMBSTONE OF THE LIVING PERSON

I just threw a lot of history at you. But history tells us a lot about where we are in the current cycle.

What is not discussed enough is the fact that, for many years, the market went nowhere. When the tech bubble[33] burst in the year 2000, the market fell by 50 percent into 2002. The market didn't recover those lost prices until 2007, at which time the market proceeded to drop once again, this time by more than half. And while stocks started to go back up again in 2009, it wasn't until 2013 that the market reached this level again and finally broke through the ceiling.

Think about that. From 2000 to 2013, if you were in the market the whole time and never sold, there was no net growth, and investors who were relying on that saw zero net return. But then things took off after 2013. Were you wondering why the last secular bear market in the table on the previous page reads "2000" with no end date? Just like when some older folks pre-purchase their tombstone and put it on the cemetery plot when they are still alive?

Because the $64,000 question is, "Has it ended yet?" Wall Street wants you to think it has, but that shouldn't come as any surprise.

STOCK MARKET PROGNOSTICATORS

Most people don't know this, but Wall Street's main business isn't selling stocks. It's selling optimism. As any salesman can tell you, no one is in the business of selling a particular commodity. Every salesman is trying to pitch you a new idealized version of yourself if you'll just buy what they're selling. In other words, they're in the business of selling dreams.

Wall Street loves to use complicated lingo to overwhelm the average investor. Consequently, I need to explain, clarify, and turn into simple, plain English the concept of Secular versus Cyclical Market Cycles.[34]

When you watch a market analyst on TV, how long does he generally imply a bear market lasts? Two to three years, right? You'll sometimes hear them say less, but rarely is it more.

As just mentioned, a full bull-bear cycle tends to last 35 years with it a 20-year or so bear market followed by a shorter bull market.

The question becomes: Who is right and who is wrong? Can both of us be right? Do you think there can be different interpretations of the same history?

Absolutely. The answer lies in how you define bear markets.

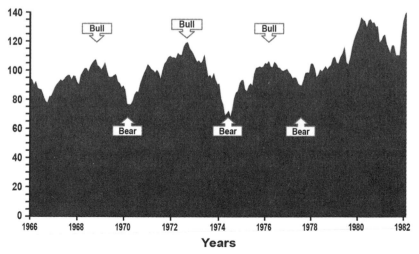

S&P 500 Secular Bear Markets 1966 - 1982

Chart D

Let's look at the 1966 to 1982 bear market as an illustration.

The cycles I labeled on this chart are what your typical analyst would call textbook bear and bull markets. They are often referred to by the industry as "cyclical" or short-term trends. My clients tell me almost daily that, in the real world, when their hard-earned dollars experience zero growth for 16 years, it's really one big bear-market cycle. So, based upon my real-world definition, a "secular" or long-term bear-market cycle averages 15–20 years[35] or longer within a larger 35-year secular bull-bear cycle.

In other words, within every secular bull or bear market there are cyclical cycles that go both up and down. For example, another way to think about a cyclical bull market inside of a secular bear market is to imagine a home with central air-conditioning and just one room with a space heater. Sure, the space heater might heat the surrounding area, but if you travel outside that vicinity, the air-conditioning will dominate the overall space.

Given this understanding, why is it that Wall Street prefers to speak in terms of textbook cyclical instead of real-world secular bull and bear markets? As you can probably figure out for yourself, they would have a hard time getting people to put their money in the market if they told them a secular bear market was upon us and that it would persist for years with zero net growth.

Simply put, focusing on shorter-term cycles allows Wall Street to speak more optimistically about the market more often. If they can persuade you that bad times will be short-lived, you'll most likely try to power through. But what I'm telling you is that the opposite is really the case.

We are still in what I consider to be a secular bear market, although we're in the late innings of the game. Granted, the rules have changed slightly since the Federal Reserve injected the markets with artificially low interest rates to keep the economy rolling (we'll discuss this more in Chapter 5). Even so, the principles remain the same.

When you're young, you've got time to lose; as you start getting older, you don't. It's as simple as that.

If time is not on your side, you don't have money to risk. Period. No ifs, ands, or buts. Remember the two major drops from this century took seven and six years to recover, respectively, and there is no law saying that the next couldn't take longer. If you want to retire within the next 10 years, or if you are already retired, you need to think very carefully before you risk one red cent of your hard-earned money investing in stocks. Better yet, don't do it at all.

I know what I'm saying might sound radical, extreme, even crazy. Trust me, I was called all three in 1999 when I got my clients out of the market, and I've been called more creative things since.

I realize it goes against the status quo to call investing in the stock market after a certain age gambling, but that's what it is.

HISTORY DOESN'T LIE

There's something else going on that I've understood for many years, and it's what I tell every client who walks through my door: If we don't see another 40 percent move down in the market, at least, it will be the first time in history we've broken three world-record milestones regarding the market, which is a situation that's very unlikely.

Let me explain myself.

WORLD RECORD #1

I talked earlier about this thing called a "secular bear market." It's a situation where several smaller bear markets happen over the course of two or three decades.

One example is the period of 1929 to 1954. Following the secular *bull* market of the Roaring '20s, the markets broke down in late October 1929, ushering in the Great Depression[36] and the worst period of economic inactivity our country has ever seen. Markets took 25 years to recover.

It's easily the best example of a secular bear market we have on record, but it's far from out of the ordinary, and we've seen many more just like it.

The important thing to remember is that, as mentioned, these secular bear markets tend to last anywhere from two to three decades. The shortest one on record lasted 16.8 years.

That's world record number one. If history proves that this secular bear market actually ended in 2013, when the market recovered its losses from its highs in 2000 and 2007, it will be the shortest secular bear market on record, lasting just 13 years.

WORLD RECORD #2

That brings me to world record number two: Every secular bear market in history has had at least three major drops.[37]

This has nothing to do with numerology or the significance of the number three. It's the simple fact that every secular bear market in history has had three major drops. It's a pattern that repeats, and if you understand anything about the stock market and human nature, it's that history repeats itself. Markets are nothing if not cyclical. In Chapter 5, I refer to it as "waves of capitulation" and explain why they recur throughout history.

Look at the secular bear market of 1929 to 1954.

The Dow Jones Industrial Average[38] collapsed by more than 80 percent from its peak of 381 in 1929 to its trough of 41 in 1932. That year, it staged a recovery for five years, quadrupling in 1937. Then, over the next five years, it fell another 50 percent, and that wasn't the final round. From 1942 to 1946, the market doubled, but then it fell by roughly 40 percent again, bottoming out for the final time in 1949. By 1954, the market finally recovered its losses from 1929 and that's before adjusting for inflation.

Dow Jones Industrial Average 1929 To 1954

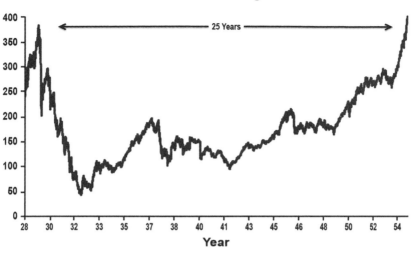

Chart E

Three crashes, three recoveries. That's what a secular bear market looks like.

To be clear, when a long-term, secular bull market ends, like the kind we saw in the 1920s, and the kind we saw in the 1980s and 1990s, it doesn't end with a whimper; it ends with a bang. One drop isn't enough; it takes decades and at least three drops for the markets to find their footing.

Let's look at the secular bear market of the 1960s and 1970s as another example.

This one was much less chaotic than the crash that sent a tidal wave over the economy between 1929 and 1932. From 1966 to 1982, the market crashed by more than 60 percent. But of course, it didn't fall in one fell swoop. The next chart puts it into perspective. (See Chart F on the following page.)

This time, we saw *five* separate crashes and five separate recoveries before the market finally reached escape velocity and overcame its 1966 peak. Each time, the market fell by more than 20 percent.

It's important to note that those first three waves down grew progressively worse.

In the first bear market, the market fell 25 percent. The next one was down 36 percent, and the third crashed 45 percent. Once again, the market had to find its footing, and even after that third crash, it took two more crashes of 27 percent and 24 percent for the secular bear market to finally end.

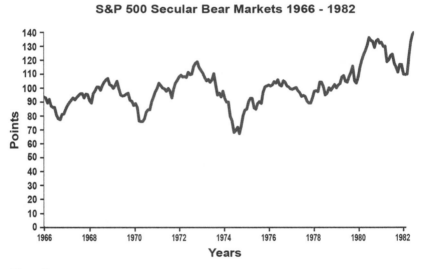

Chart F

So as you see, secular bear markets are carnage incarnate. You do not want to own stocks when you're in the midst of one. The trick, of course, is knowing when these secular bear markets end, and that's easier said than done, since no one, not even myself, can time the market perfectly.

I can tell you this, however. I pulled most of my clients out of the market in 1999 *before* the tech bubble burst. I sent a message to my clients in the fall of 2007 warning them that another crash was coming soon and that it was going to be bigger than the first. Sure enough, the market peaked in October of that year.

More recently, I've intentionally stayed out of the stock market during the last few years and missed out on what is the "Trump Bump," and I'm okay with that. At 53 years old, I don't feel a day over 40, and I have a lot fewer gray hairs than I would have otherwise had I'd stayed in stocks and kept my clients in stocks.

But I'm convinced, beyond a shadow of a doubt, that a third drop is coming. History has shown us the probability.

I haven't even gotten to the third and final world record that we would have broken, if we are indeed already out of the woods and into the next secular bull market.

The first is that the shortest secular bear market on record lasted just 16.8 years. The second is that each one had at least three drops. The third is that, in each secular bear market, P/E ratios have always fallen into the single digits before the market staged a recovery.

WORLD RECORD #3

Let me say that again. We have never in history recovered from a secular bear market without P/E ratios falling into the single digits.

P/E ratios are a big reason why I was so confident about my prediction of a market drop in the late 1990s.

You see, every stock has a P/E or price-to-earnings ratio, as does the entire stock market. The formula is relatively simple:

P/E = Price Per Share/Earnings Per Share

As a general rule of thumb, if you are comparing two stocks in the same industry, the one with the lower ratio is probably a better buy because it is considered to be "undervalued." For example:

Company A: Stock price of $30 per share
           Corporate earnings of $1 per share

Company B: Stock price of $50 per share
           Corporate earnings of $5 per share

Which one is the better value? Company B, because it has a P/E of 10 compared to Company A's P/E of 30.

Company A: P/E = $30/$1 = 30

Company B: P/E = $50/$5 = 10

Price-per-share and earnings-per-share ratios of the overall stock market are an important indicator for how much room the stock market has to grow. For example, every secular bear market in history has ended only when P/E ratios drop into the single digits—in fact, historically, this has been a reliable indicator that the next secular bull market was afoot. Conversely, when they get too high, in the mid-20s or higher, there's generally only one way they can go—down, as the next secular bear market emerges. This was the case in the late 1990s when average P/E ratios had exceeded 30. In other words, each dollar invested was buying 3 cents of earnings of annual profits (1/30= 3.3). Put another way, you were earning about 3 percent when you could have taken the same money and bought an FDIC-insured CD back then with no risk that was paying 5 percent.

Now, P/E ratios are nothing like they were at the top of the tech bubble when the average stock traded at 44 times earnings,[39] and not even quite at the level of insanity we saw in 1929. But they are still the third highest in U.S. history.

It doesn't mean a crash will happen tomorrow, but when our greatest source of comfort is in knowing that today's P/E ratios haven't hit the levels of financial insanity as the two moments of our greatest collective stupidity, we're in trouble.

CAN WE REALLY BEAT THREE WORLD RECORDS?

Point is, we have never gotten through a secular bear-market cycle without P/E ratios falling into the single digits.

And we haven't seen them yet in the current secular cycle.

Look at the chart below.

As you can see, in every secular bear market, P/E ratios bottomed out in the single digits.

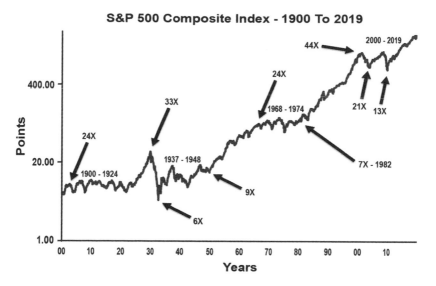

Chart G

The closest we've come to that in the current cycle was in 2009, when P/E ratios dropped to 13 times that of earnings. You start to understand why that drop was historically bound to happen when you realize that, following the tech bubble burst, P/E ratios only dropped to 21 times that of earnings. Again, none of this stuff is a guarantee that the market will crash tomorrow, but it begs some questions.

Do you believe history repeats itself? Do you believe proven historical patterns are just coincidence? Do you think this time is *really* different? Are you really willing to make that bet?

Maybe we've broken all of these world records due to the Federal Reserve's unprecedented manipulation of the U.S. financial markets. Only time will tell.

I'll tell you this—7 of the 10 people who walk through my door end up becoming a client after I present this evidence to them. I fear for the other 30 percent.

To conclude this point, let's quickly revisit those three world records.

Number One: The shortest secular bear market on record lasted 16.8 years between 1966 and 1982. This time, the market reclaimed its year 2000 peak in just 13 years—unless we have another crash.[40]

Number Two: Every secular bear market in history has had at least three major drops. Some have had four, five, or six, but each one of them has had at least three drops and three recoveries. This time we have only had two.[41]

Number Three: We've never recovered from a secular bear market without P/E ratios getting down into the single digits. P/E ratios have to get down into the single digits to justify a recovery, and that hasn't happened yet either.

In fact, P/E ratios have been above their long-term average for all but *seven months* since 1991.[42]

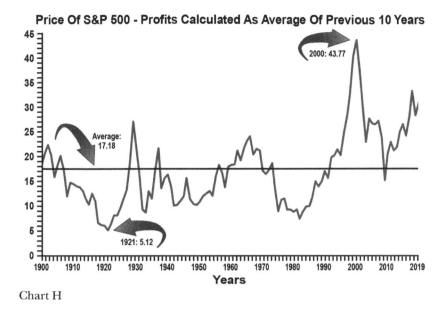

Chart H

THE $64,000 QUESTION

So, do you think it's possible that we have broken those three world records and recovered from that last secular bear market in 2013?

If you are thinking, "Well, technically, anything is possible," then I believe the important question is, "Historically speaking, is it probable?"

Well, a few things would probably have to be in place in order for that to happen.

For one, we'd have to have the best economy we've ever seen. We'd have to have wages that haven't stagnated for 30 years. We'd have to have a national debt level that doesn't surpass our annual GDP, with the GDP[43] level being the highest our country has ever seen. We would have to have strong trade pacts with our allies. We'd have to have a thriving middle class. We'd have to have a labor force participation rate that hasn't been rapidly collapsing for the last 20 years. We'd have to see corporations putting their money toward productive means rather than using it to artificially inflate their stock prices.

Unfortunately, though, none of these things are true; and every one of them today creates a headwind to higher stock prices.

At this point, I'm sure a lot of you reading this can tell something's not right with this picture. But let's say I didn't convince you with the three world records.[44] Let's say you need tangible evidence that isn't rooted in historical patterns and numerology.

To that, I'm happy to oblige.

HOW YOU CAN INVEST YOUR MONEY

So, Dave, I get it, you are telling me not to gamble; but are you saying that if I'm not a business owner or a billionaire that I can't be an investor?

Of course not; when you buy bonds and bond-like instruments, it's completely different.

When you buy a bond, you're actually investing. Better yet, you're investing by contract.

Here's what I mean. When you buy a bond, it typically comes with two sets of guarantees from the issuer:

1. A fixed rate of interest every year for the life of the bond.
2. A fixed value that will be returned to you come the maturity of the bond.

There's very little risk involved. You know how much you make. You know how much you get back. It's a contract. There's no funny math, and there's zero guesswork about what will happen. It is what it is.

That's why bonds are probably the single most boring investment on earth. But at a certain age, you want boring. You want guaranteed income. You *don't* want risk.

An analogy that I always use is—it's like real estate. If you buy properties to collect rent payments, you're investing for the income, and you are also investing by contract. That contract is called a lease agreement. You check your tenant's credit background to minimize any chance he defaults, and if he doesn't, then you know exactly what return in the form of income you will receive.

Now imagine that your tenant signs a 10-year lease with a commitment to buy at the end of the 10 years, at a fixed-market value. So the income you receive monthly is fixed for the next 10 years, as is the sales price at the end of the term. Assuming that you have done a good job on the credit check, hasn't he removed 100 percent of the risk of this transaction? of course, if you sell the lease agreement to another investor before the 10 years, you could take a loss.

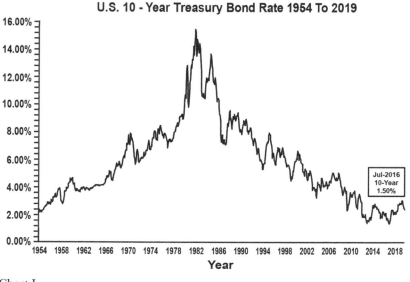

Chart I

However, if you hold it to term, you know exactly what you will receive. The transaction I just described is very much how a bond works.

WOULD YOU FLIP PROPERTIES FOR RETIREMENT INCOME?

What would make more sense if your goal was to generate retirement income for yourself now, or in the near future? Flipping properties or buying rental property? If you flip properties, you're investing for the growth; moreover, you are speculating. And you really have to do three things well to make that gamble pay off. You've got to buy it at the right time, you have to put money in the right areas and hope it goes up, and then you have to sell at the right time. Clearly it's more speculative than owning rental property where you only have to do ONE thing well— execute a solid contract with a credit-worthy tenant.

CHAPTER 5

The Problem with This Bull Market

O NE OF THE TOUGHEST things about investing is that it requires diligence and hard work. Unfortunately, when it comes to making money, most people are looking for a shortcut. It could be something they saw on the news, a stock tip they got from an uncle, or an idea they got in the shower and researched on the computer for an hour.

That's not investing. Heck, it's not even gambling.

Investing at its core is a grind. You get up early, check stocks, follow news, watch the wires, study, research, analyze, and do it again day after day.

It reminds me a lot of working out at the gym.

When I was younger, I was big into weight lifting. At an early age I had a healthy respect for people who were bigger, faster, stronger, and smarter than me. I was competitive. I wanted to be just like them.

As a teenager, I started lifting weights at home. My mom would spot me. I started out just lifting the weights we had lying around the house.

I kept at it for a couple of years and started to put on muscle. Eventually my mom said, "It's time for you to join a gym."

So I did. And I committed to it.

I said, if I'm going to do this, I'm going to do it for real. I wanted to be a national champion. I meant it, too.

I went to my first competition when I was 16. Frankly, I was too young. Most of the other teens there were either 18 or 19 years old. Still, I placed 6th out of 13.

I kept at it.

By the time I was 19, I wasn't just ready to compete. I was ready to win. And I did win. I went nuts competing and won every contest I entered. I won the teenage overall division, and then I entered the men's division and won in my weight class. There I was, 19 years old, going up against guys who were 25 to 30 years old and beating them.

Then, in 1985, I went all the way. I entered the Heavyweight Division of the Teenage National competition knowing I'd go against the best bodybuilders in the country.

I won.

After that, I quit.

I knew bodybuilding wasn't going to be the career for me. Still, I wanted to see it through to the finish line, and see it through I did. I'm glad I did. It taught me some very important lessons I carry with me to this day.

BE WARY OF STEROIDS

Namely, there are no shortcuts in life. Not in weight lifting, not in relationships, not in investing. There is no get-rich-quick scheme.

As a weight lifter, I came across a lot of guys who were experimenting with steroids in the early '80s. The thing about steroids is that they do allow you to push your body past its normal limits.

But the human body has its limitations for a reason. We now know that some of the long-term side effects of steroids include liver disease, cardiovascular complications, damage to the reproductive organs, and mood imbalance, to name a few.

The point is, steroids aren't natural. When you take them, it's like performing a lab experiment on your body.

Imagine you and I were working out and we came across a guy on steroids benching 400 pounds in the gym. We make a bet. I wager that once he goes back off the steroids he can only bench 300 pounds, and you bet 350.

Here's the thing—we're both speculating. It's a complete gamble how much he'll be able to bench once the steroids go out of his system.

But we know one thing for sure. He probably can't bench the 400 pounds without them.

So, why am I telling you all this?

The reason is that for the last 10 years we've undergone the greatest financial lab experiment in the history of mankind.

When the market dropped by half between 2000 and 2002, it was the greatest crash our country had experienced since the Great Depression. It was easily the biggest crash in our lifetimes, at the time. Most people didn't know that sort of thing was possible, especially after nearly 20 years of double-digit annual gains in the stock market.

When it happened again in 2007, only worse, it set in a panic, as you well remember. That's why government and central banks around the world resorted to experimental measures to artificially bolster the economy, prop up the stock market, and get the financial system running again.

In a very literal sense, they injected the markets with steroids. The question on everyone's mind, though, is, "How much lower will the markets drop when they go off the steroids completely?" Your guess is as good as mine.

FINANCIAL ENGINEERING

Here's the deal: Three massive forces have propped up the stock market since the year 2009. If these forces weren't at play, then the third awaited stock market drop in the secular bear-market cycle would probably have already occurred. P/E ratios[45] might have finally dropped into the single digits, the worst would be over, and we could all move on with our lives and perhaps even safely invest in the stock market as the start of a new secular bull market would likely have already arrived.

Unfortunately, there's been a ton of financial engineering at play that has artificially kept the stock market afloat, even seeming to thrive, as cracks form in the foundation.

The first force that's helped keep stocks above water is the Federal Reserve and their use of economic steroids.

I'm sure you're all familiar with this story, so I don't need to beat you over the head with it.

Suffice to say, former Federal Reserve chair Ben Bernanke[46] took an unprecedented move when he decided to slash the overnight Fed Funds Rate to zero percent during the heart of the financial crisis in 2008 and 2009. The Fed Funds Rate is the interest rate that banks charge when they lend each other money overnight and it's the interest rate upon which all other interest rates are based. When the Federal Reserve sets interest rate policy, they do it through control of this interest rate. When it falls, all other interest rates fall, and vice versa.

This artificially propped up the economy by encouraging people to borrow money, spend it, and get the economy moving. When you can borrow money at essentially zero percent interest rates, money is practically free, and who doesn't love free stuff?

But that's not all the Federal Reserve did. They also engineered a radical program called quantitative easing[47] in which they repurchased trillions of dollars' worth of U.S. Treasury bonds.

For those who have heard this term ad nauseam but don't fully understand what it is, it's when a central bank, like the Federal Reserve, introduces new money into the money supply. It's as simple as that, but the way it works is slightly complicated.

Essentially what the Fed started doing was buying a whole bunch of Treasuries from other banks, thereby artificially inflating their demand, driving long-term interest rates downward and injecting a ton of cash into the capital markets.

Where did the Fed get the money to purchase these assets? They simply created it out of thin air. Central banks[48] alone have this unique power.

The idea was that a larger money supply, combined with lower short and long-term interest rates, would encourage banks to make more loans and, in turn, allow consumers and business owners to take on more debt, refinance their homes, start or expand businesses, and so on. There was just one problem: People, for a long-time, weren't dumb enough to take the bait.

Homeowners, investors, and the like weren't exactly jumping out of their seats to take on more debt, even at near zero percent interest rates, because they had just barely survived the worst financial crisis we'd seen in our lifetimes. That's why it took the Federal Reserve three rounds of quantitative easing (four if you count Operation Twist,[49] which, essentially, was quantitative easing under a different brand) to get a modicum of an effect. Between 2008 and 2015, the Fed's balance sheet ballooned from $900 billion to $4.5 trillion. In other words, they bought back $3.6 trillion in debt to get the economy moving from a dead stop to a slow crawl.

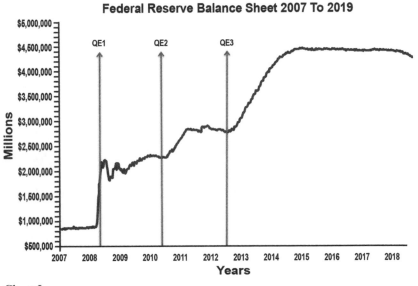

Chart J

It was a controversial program. Lots of people think it worked, and it did depending on how you slice it. After all, we're a lot better off today than we were at the bottom of the financial crisis in 2008.

However, I don't think anyone in their right mind truly believes you can just "create" money out of thin air and not have to pay for it later. My suspicion, and the suspicion of many others, is that we've simply "delayed" the worst effects of the financial crisis. Eventually, the chickens have to come home to roost. The cracks in our economy haven't gone away; we just put a Band-Aid over a gaping wound, gave ourselves a pat on the back, and walked away. We didn't *fundamentally* fix anything.

STEROIDS DO HAVE SIDE EFFECTS

What did responsible individuals do with the extra money supply if they didn't spend it? They saved or invested it. And with lower interest rates, investors were tempted to move up the risk curve and pour more money into the stock market as other interest-bearing alternatives appeared less attractive.

There's another effect as well. Quantitative easing also puts a ceiling on the value of our currency. This makes the stock market more attractive to foreign investors.

The result? A stock market recovery that was much greater than the underlying economic recovery, and a larger-than-ever disparity between economic classes in our country.

FINANCIAL ENGINEERING PART II

So, there are three forces that have kept the stock market trucking along. The first was the Federal Reserve's economic steroids. The second is margin debt levels, and it's a direct result of the first.

Margin debt is debt an investor, business, or corporation takes on by trading on margin. It's applying leverage to boost your re-turns without having to put as much capital at stake, at least at first.

Perhaps you've done this in the past. When purchasing stocks or bonds through a broker, investors have the option to place the trade through a cash account, where they buy the asset in full, or via a margin account, in which they put up a small portion—say one-fifth of the overall price—and borrow the rest from the bro-ker. The leftover portion is known as margin debt.

Think of it like a 20 percent down payment on a house, except in the financial markets. Not many people have between $300,000 and $500,000 sitting around to buy a physical asset like a home, and a home is a daily survival need. So, we have mortgages that allow us to put up a small sum, a down payment, to partially own the house and pay off the rest over 10, 20, or 30 years, plus interest. It makes sense that we have this option available to us, because, again, people need homes.

What margin debt does is it takes that exact same formula and applies it to non-physical assets in the financial markets (which I think you and I can probably agree aren't exactly necessary for survival, but I won't split hairs).

You can see where a problem might arise.

If you have $50,000 and borrow $200,000 to purchase 1,250 shares of Amazon at $2,000 per share, you have $250,000 in liabilities. But you only *have* $50,000.

If Amazon's stock drops to $1,500, which, as we've learned, can happen in the span of a couple months, you're out $62,500. Since you only had $50,000 to begin with, in other words, you now *owe* $12,500.

On the other hand, if Amazon's stock were to rise to $3,000, you could cash out for $375,000, pay back your $200,000 in margin debt, and still have $175,000. Your profit—$125,000 on a $50,000 investment before interest.

Who doesn't love the sound of that? It probably gets you excited just reading that.

However, it doesn't always work out that way. As we know, the growth can always turn into a big fat loss (and I'll say it a few more times before this book is over).

This is where it gets really scary. Not just scary, but completely out-of-this-world insane.

Look at how out of control our margin debt levels have grown over the past 22 years.

As you can plainly see from the chart on the following page, margin debt levels have progressively grown higher and higher with each consecutive crash.

They peaked in March 2000. That month, the benchmark technology index, the Nasdaq, peaked. Then the overall market crashed 50 percent. The Nasdaq[50] fell 80 percent.

Chart K

Margin debt levels peaked again in July 2007, this time much higher. Three months later, the stock market peaked and proceeded to crash by 58 percent.

Today, margin debt levels are higher than they've ever been and are looking very, very shaky, and this should concern you because for the last two crashes, when margin debt levels started to fall, the stock market fell right alongside them.

The chart on the top of the following page overlays margin debt levels with the credit balances in the customers' securities margin accounts over the last 20 or so years to show exactly what I mean.

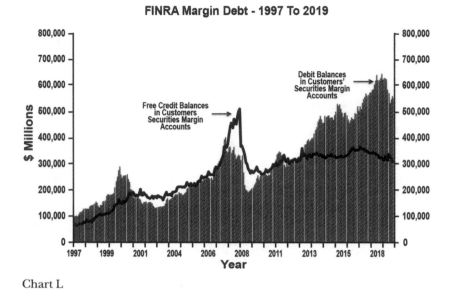

Chart L

FINANCIAL ENGINEERING PART III

The third and final piece of the puzzle that has kept the market surging ever higher is the corporate buyback.

In a buyback, corporations repurchase shares of their own stock to limit the number of shares on the open market, thereby increasing the value of each remaining share. Since the CEO's job is to increase the value of the company's shares for its shareholders, this is one quick and easy tactic that can raise share prices without fundamentally growing the company or reinvesting in the business. It's fine here and there, but it's quite frankly been abused in recent years.

Apple Inc.[51] was the first company to hit the $1 trillion mile mark, so I'll use them as an example of what this looks like.

Apple has roughly five billion shares in the open market. At a $1 trillion valuation, those shares would be worth $200 apiece. But Apple's management and board of directors have a fiduciary duty to their shareholders to increase the value of Apple's stock.

Since Apple hasn't come out with a new or original product in a quite a while, their share price has been kept afloat by regurgitating the same product over and over until, lo and behold, it no longer works. They also do it through stock buybacks.

With five billion available shares, let's say they just repurchase 100 million shares, or 2 percent of the total shares outstanding. That leaves $1 trillion in valuation divided across 4.9 billion remaining shares. Each share is now worth $204.08, or an increase of roughly 2 percent for every shareholder of Apple's stock.

It sounds innocent enough, until you realize that these stock buybacks account for a significant portion of the market's gains since 2008. Since the heart of the financial crisis, U.S. corporations have spent over $5.1 trillion buying back their own stock. It has been widely documented that the single biggest buyer of U.S. stocks has been U.S. corporations themselves. That's a problem.

This chart illustrates how corporate buybacks move in lockstep with the stock market. Corporations repurchase shares of their own stock to keep the market moving.

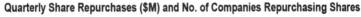

Quarterly Share Repurchases ($M) and No. of Companies Repurchasing Shares

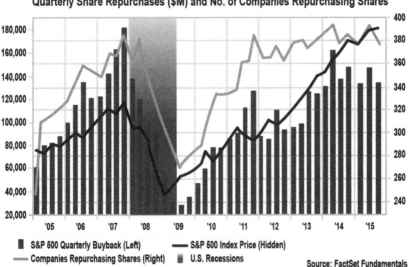

Chart M

When you put all three pieces of the puzzle together, it creates a clear picture as to why the stock market is not sustainable at today's prices.

First, the Federal Reserve slashed interest rates to zero, making it virtually free to borrow money. That allowed individuals to increase their margin debt levels to record highs and corporations to borrow money to buy back shares; all having the effect of pushing stock prices up even further.

What you have then is an artificially inflated stock market propped up on little more than financial engineering.

If you know anything about addiction, you understand that it takes more and more of a drug to get the same effect the longer you're addicted to it. Eventually, the drug stops having an effect altogether, and then one day you overdose trying desperately to get that high.

Here's the full picture.

Assuming you participated 100 percent of the time, we had the greatest bull market in U.S. history in the 1980s and 1990s. From 2000 to 2013, the market gained absolutely no ground. Since then, most of the market's gains can be attributed to financial engineering on behalf of our central banks and corporations.

This is not the stuff that a secular bull market is made of. It is the sign of an addict refusing to come to terms with their addiction.

My belief is that the only reason this cyclical (or short-term) bull market has gone on for as long as it is because U.S. stocks have been the best game in town. While investors can still get a 3 percent yield on U.S. Treasuries, government bonds around the world are in *negative* territory. In Japan and in Europe, they're still experimenting with negative interest rates to boost their economies. Zero wasn't even good enough. Then Trump got elected, and we got the so-called "Trump bump." That's why the market rose so much in 2017.

What's the next "fix" going to be? How long can the gravy train keep rolling until we run into a wall? I can't say for certain, but I believe that eventually the third drop has to come.

Yes, we've started going off of our drug. Quantitative easing is technically over; the Federal Reserve has raised short-term rates off of zero, and it is still in the process of selling some of the $3.6 trillion worth of bonds they added to their balance sheet, but at a snail's pace. And based on recent volatility, that may be a good thing. If you've ever met an addict, you know that coming off an addiction is never easy. There's almost always a comedown.

THE THIRD CRASH

So this helps explain why that third stock market drop hasn't happened yet, and let's face it, some laboratory experiments end successfully while others end in explosion. Time will tell with this one, but even with a successful outcome, nothing changes the fact that we have almost 200 years of stock market history, which indicates that a third drop in this secular bear market is very likely. In fact, history implies that stock market levels have to get back down to where they were at their peaks in 2000, 2007, and 2013. From today's levels, as of this writing, that represents a minimum of a 40 percent drop. But it could be much, much worse.

Think back to the last secular bear-market cycle between 1966 and 1982 for context.

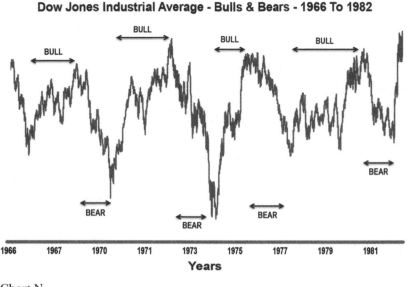

Chart N

Notice the first major drop that occurred during this 16-year cycle. Now look at the second drop. Now look at the third.

Do you notice a pattern?

What's plainly evident in this chart is that each drop was larger than the previous one, causing waves of anxiety that prompted investors to sell more with each consecutive drop. The third drop was the biggest, by no small point of coincidence. From the Holy Trinity to patterns in nature, things happen in threes. There were drops that occurred after the third, but they were smaller in magnitude. Although a wave pattern like this doesn't always occur in a secular bear market, it is common for these to come in sets of threes with the third drop being the largest. This phenomenon tends to rear its ugly head more frequently than some Wall Street analysts care to admit.

As you can tell from my tone, waves may make pretty charts, but they are not positive phenomena when it comes to either your money or your psyche as an investor.

There are lots of so-called "wave theories" that attempt to explain these patterns, most of which are extremely complicated. I'd like to give you what I believe is the simplest explanation that you'll ever hear.

WHY A THIRD DROP IS LIKELY

The first drop is usually a clear indication that the good times are over. During the secular bull-market cycle, market dips were short and typically not too severe. Once a decisive break below support levels indicates an end of the bull market, from there it's a matter of guessing how long the bad times will last as investors try to call a bottom in the market.

After the first drop in 1966, Wall Street advised people to "hang in there and don't sell." Conventional wisdom explained, "You can't time the market." As a result, when the first market drop occurred, many investors acted like wooden soldiers. They dutifully sat on the sidelines and held onto their stocks. The market recovered and the mini-crisis was averted. Investors experienced a period of market calm. The pro-market prognosticators smiled.

A couple years went by and eventually more bad news arrived that caused a second drop. During good times, this bad news would have manifested itself as merely a blip and the stock market would have bounced back. I believe that because it came so soon after the first drop, this one was more severe.

This time, several years passed with investors becoming frustrated with market losses and/or a lack of expected gains. Many became impatient. The average investor started to sell, which caused the market to slide in a second period of decline in the secular bear-market cycle. Because there were more people selling into this second drop, the second drop was, as is often the case, bigger than the first.

More years went by. Eventually, the market recovered. There was a period of calm. Inevitably, more bad news arrived. Again, it was the type of news markets would have simply brushed off during the good times. Because the market had gone so long without any significant progress, it resulted in a third and even worse crash.

At this time, because so many investors had given up and cashed in their chips, only the most patient and stalwart investors were still in the market. However, even these investors had grown so impatient that eventually they started to capitulate and sell into the third drop. With more sellers than ever before, the third drop became worse than the first and second.

WHERE ARE WE NOW?

As I'm writing this book in the spring of 2019, we've been in one of the longest cyclical bull markets in history[52] thanks to unprecedented levels of financial engineering, quantitative easing, artificially low interest rates, corporate buybacks, and other shenanigans.

Some believe the market will continue to go up and that we've reached what is known as "escape velocity." This is when a rocket escapes the resistance of earth's atmosphere and thrusts headlong into space where there is no gravity to fight against its upward momentum.

I'm skeptical that we can overcome 200 years of stock market history that says a third drop is likely, that we can get through a secular bear-market cycle in record time without the third drop, and without P/E ratios in the single digits.

I realize the last two decades of investing haven't been easy. The two drops we've seen so far this century have significantly handicapped the retirement plans of most Americans. My hope is that this book will help you make sense of the madness and make you realize there is a better way.

What it comes down to is the fact that we are living in a brand-new age of economic uncertainty, one in which many of the old textbook rules and guidelines for investing and retirement planning have become outdated, if not downright contradicting the many rules and "guidelines" often pushed to retail investors. Adding to that fact is the need for new rules and strategies and the host of financial challenges unique to today's generation of retirees and near-retirees, challenges that our parents and grandparents didn't face. These include the near-disappearance of defined benefit pension plans, the ever-rising cost of healthcare, the fact that many people near retirement age are caring for aging parents and/or grown children, and the reality that life expectancy rates are higher than ever, meaning that people need to prepare for at least 30 years of reliable retirement income.

Many people are taught that in order to increase your returns you must increase your growth through old-fashioned buy and hold stock market strategies. However, they *aren't* taught that this approach doesn't work in a long-term secular bear-market cycle like the one we're in now.

So my point is this: If you don't want to invest in the income, because you've got a $1-million-per-year pension and you're only spending $100K a year, then maybe you invest in the "I" because you want to be a good steward of your money and you want to protect it.

Remember, income is just a component of return. It's an alternative to growth. You don't need to invest for the "G." If you do, you might get a 40 percent hit. Alternatively, if you invest for the "I," you're protected, and you get a more consistent return.

That's the whole point.

What it all comes down to, for you, is this: Do you really want to bet that there won't be another drop in the next two to three years, knowing the secular bear markets tend to last 20 years or more, and knowing that the market has been propped up by trillions of dollars' worth of economic steroids and financial engineering?

Can you really bet that the bull market will be around for the rest of your life? Can you afford, at this point in your life, to take another 40 percent hit? Or do you think you'd be better off settling for a safer, more consistent income goal of 4 to 5 percent every year, knowing it might actually leave you better off than if you left your money in the market?

CHAPTER 6

Stock Market Addiction

THERE'S A STORY I like to tell my colleagues and clients, a parable, if you will, about a little girl who doesn't understand why her mother cuts the ends off of the roast before she sticks it in the oven. From the daughter's point of view, it seems like wasting a perfectly good slice of meat.

"Mom, why do you cut the ends off the roast?" the daughter eventually asks.

The mother replies, "Because, sweetie, that's the way we've always done it. It's the way your grandma did it."

The daughter, unsatisfied, asks, "But *why*?"

Her mother, with a clear answer, responds, "Well, we're going to grandma's house this weekend. When we get there, you can ask her."

That weekend, they go to grandma's house and the little girl asks, "Grandma, why do we cut the ends off the roast before we put it in the oven?"

The grandma laughs and says, "Oh, honey, I haven't done that in years. I used to do that when your mom was little because back then our roasting pan was so small we had to cut the ends off to make it fit."

This parable illustrates a prescient fact—humans are creatures of habit. We have a tendency to repeat our behavior, even when it defies rational logic and we've forgotten why we do what we do in the first place. It shows how our earliest experiences shape our paradigms, whether or not they make sense.

It's the same when it comes to investing.

Our generation's earliest investing experience was during the single greatest bull market in U.S. history. In 1980, the Dow was at 700. By the year 2000, it had climbed to 11,700, a 16-fold increase.

Back then, you couldn't lose money investing in stocks. Annual returns of 15 to 20 percent became the new math. P/E ratios of 100 times that of earnings or more became normal. We rationalized it until it blew up in our faces. But even after two crashes it doesn't matter, because that was our first paradigm.[53] We're still cutting the ends off the roast because we don't know any better.

We've forgotten that total return has *two* components, the income and the growth, and it's no wonder why.

Our generation was led into the best bull market in U.S. history with the perfect storm: the onset of 401(k)s and the emerging popularity of mutual funds. No longer was the stock market exclusively for the affluent; it had become a place for the average investor. Since investing in individual stocks in 401(k)s required too much research, the popularity of mutual funds skyrocketed. Now, investing in "the market" had become so simple that anyone could do it and anyone did. With more money flowing into the market than ever before, it rose faster, causing investors to speculate even more, and the cycle was off and running.

Fortunately, thanks to the sheer magnitude of that bull run, the average investor did very well, at least for a while. Suddenly, we started to believe that anyone could become rich, that everyone could achieve the American Dream, and with the rise of 401(k)s and the ease of mutual funds, it seemed more than possible.

By the late 1990s, we had become a country of investors addicted to stocks and stock mutual funds. The young lady at the checkout register and the young man stocking shelves would spend their break time debating whether eBay or Amazon.com had more upside potential. TV shows dedicated to the stock market became more and more popular as everyone wanted a piece of that American Dream. Many began to forget that they were speculating, gambling, if you will, and thought they were mini–Warren Buffetts.

Then, beginning in Y2K,[54] everything began to change. As we discussed in Chapter 3, for the next nearly 14 years, the market was underwater and struggled to get back to even. But that hasn't broken our addiction to stocks. The funny thing about addiction, and the behaviors that form from our earliest paradigms, is that we continue to give into our addictions even as history proves it can be bad for you.

HABITS DIE HARD

In 1999, when I was convinced the market was too frothy, I started pulling my clients' money out of the market BEFORE the first drop. And you better believe me when I say I pulled it out kicking and screaming. These were the end of the so-called "good ol' days" when stocks would double in a day simply by adding the words "dot com" at the end of their name, the days when you'd talk to bellhops and store clerks who were getting "rich" off high-flying tech stocks. People were out of their minds. The party was hot and no one wanted it to end. No one believed it could.

Months later, when the market crashed, I received a small cartful of letters from clients thanking me for quite literally saving their financial lives, after their money had grown exponentially in the bull market and I pulled them out near the top.

Ever since, I've dedicated my financial career to focusing on the "I," the income, because I realized the "G" was broken. And from what I know of economics, I knew it would be broken for some time—years, if not decades.

Still, there are lots of people who don't want to make the switch. And I understand why.

Human beings are creatures of habit. We don't like change. Which is why, when a new client walks in my door and I start talking about radically altering their financial strategy to focus on the "I" and kicking stocks to the curb, I'm often met with a bit of resistance. But it's not because what I'm saying doesn't make sense. It's because they haven't heard it before.

After all, our generation was raised on the glorious days of the '80s and '90s bull market when stocks were a sure thing. That's our paradigm. It's our reality.

But investing for income isn't some newfangled concept.

After all, it's what did our parents' generation did. Most who retired in the 20th century had social security and some sort of pension. They had income. They weren't depending on their 401(k)s to fund the majority of their retirement expenses. When the stock market changed the tide in the year 2000 onward, it may have affected them emotionally, but it didn't force them to change their lifestyles, because they still had income.

It's different with our generation.

Those who retired in the last few years are depending more and more on their investments to fulfill basic needs. Without the proper income, many are utilizing the withdrawal method, and are lucky in that they haven't been doing it long enough to risk running out of money yet. Worse, many have "enabled" their stock-addicted portfolios by working longer or making drastic lifestyle changes to temporarily reduce the withdrawals needed, but that can't last forever. The problem is that the more money you withdraw, the less income you can generate, and the less money you'll have when you actually need it. Then the double whammy—so long as your money is in stocks or stock mutual funds, you risk getting wiped out the next time the market takes a hit. So again, what I'm advocating isn't some new idea, it's actually about implementing the prudence from our parent's generation so you never risk running out of money. This is about getting back to basics so you don't have to take those risks I just mentioned. It's about doing what our parents did, and their parents before them, and not letting our culture's addiction to stocks allow us to forget a simple truth: when you are at or near retirement age, and risking your money in the market, you are gambling with time. Stocks are the casino, and the years of your life remaining are your chips.

WHY HAS NO ONE EVER TOLD ME THIS?

If this sounds new to you, let's face it, most of us didn't have a lot money invested in the markets before 1980. That was 40 years ago. Our generation doesn't know what investing for the "I" looks like. We've only been taught the "G."

But this is where a keen understanding of history helps. Do you remember how many years it takes for a full secular bull-bear cycle to unfold?[55] Nearly 40 years. This means that most investors today haven't yet experienced all four seasons of the stock market.

Imagine if you were moving from sunny Florida to frigid Maine in the late spring or early summer. Could you really know what to expect in the winter? of course not. You haven't experienced all four seasons yet.

In life, don't our earliest experiences in any realm shape our paradigms?

Most investors today were raised during the glorious days of the 1980s and 1990s bull market when stocks rose 15 percent, on average, every year. The long-term average is roughly 8 percent. That means for almost 20 years the market was nearly doubling its average annual return.

When the first 10 or 20 years of your experience as an investor starts with 15 percent annual returns, you don't forget it. It programs you to expect above-average returns even if, for the next 20 years, your average return never comes close to that. Case in point, the average annual return of the S&P 500[56] from the market top in early 2000 through the end of 2018 is less than 3 percent.* It went from doubling the long-term average to less than half. But that's why long-term averages only tell half the story.

OPTIMISM

Back in May of 2009, the University of Kansas and Gallup presented a study at the Association for Psychological Science[57] on whether humans are more optimistic or pessimistic by nature. It was 2009, mind you, and people had just come out of the worst economic hit since the Great Depression and had no idea at that point that the worst was over.

Yet, the study, a sample of 150,000 adults that is representative of approximately 95 percent of the world population, found that the majority, 89 percent, expected the next five years to be as good or better than their current life, and that 95 percent of them expected their life to be as good or better at the end of those five years.

These results show overwhelming evidence that mankind is optimistic by nature.

No doubt, there are plenty of benefits to being optimistic. Imagine the cancer patient that loses the battle but remains

---

*Price Return Only. Dividents not included.

hopeful until the very end. The sports fan who enters every season thinking his team will win the championship this year even though they've never come close. The lottery ticket buyer who has bought 1,000 lottos and still remains hopeful. The stock speculator who lost money on his last dozen trades but is going for lucky number 13.

Sure, in many cases, optimism is a good thing. Studies show that optimistic people tend to live longer. They have an easier time making friends and attracting romantic partners. They also tend to be more charismatic. But optimism isn't all sunshine and roses. The downside of optimism is that people tend to downplay the negatives even in the face of evidence.

As discussed, a secular bear market, defined as an extended period of volatility and zero net growth, often lasts 20 years or longer. So let me ask you: Do you think that during each of those secular bear cycles, 100 percent of investors eventually pulled 100 percent of their money out of the markets? of course not—many stayed invested. It wasn't the pessimists who knew bad times could get worse, but the optimists who always thought recovery was right around the corner.

Again, it's one thing if you're young and still in the accumulation phase of your career. If you're in the income phase, you can't afford to let your bias toward optimism influence the financial decisions that affect your livelihood.

INVESTING THROUGH THE REARVIEW MIRROR

Fortunately, due to heroic government and central bank efforts, the U.S. stock market surpassed its previous high set in 2000 and began to skyrocket again in 2013. As highlighted in Chapter 4, during the next four to five years, the stock market nearly doubled. And from its 2009 lows, it quadrupled.

Psychologists would say that this is where recency bias kicks in, the tendency to extrapolate the recent past out into the future. That means that if the market is falling, one thinks it will continue to fall. If it's rising, it will continue to rise. I call this "investing through the rearview mirror" because it skews our perception and takes our attention away from what really matters. Unfortunately, the rearview mirror isn't even the mirror that lets you see that far behind, but rather your side-view mirror, with the warning label "objects may be closer than they appear."

Optimism plays a role in this, too. For many investors, when the markets are shrinking, optimism can overpower our recency bias, at least in the early stages of a bear market. When markets are climbing, optimism and recency bias team up to blind even the most rational investors.

GROWTH VERSUS RETURN

I realize it's hard to quit stocks when they're hot, or at any time really. When you're up, you want to ride the wave higher. When you're down, you hope stocks will turn around so you can make up for lost ground. It's the same sort of addiction that affects drug users, smokers, gamblers, you name it.

We need to remember an important point—whether you're investing for growth or investing for income, at the end of the day, there's only one thing we're all looking for, and that's a return on our investment.

We have now been in a cyclical, short-term bull market for more than 10 years since we came off the bottom in 2009. For many investors, it feels like a hallmark to the '80s and '90s. All they can think about is the "G," and it shows. Several times a week, an investor, retired or approaching retirement, will tell me that they are looking for growth on their money.

What they fail to remember is that growth is just one of

the avenues for seeking return. It doesn't have to be the end-all-be-all.

To illustrate this, I usually pitch a hypothetical scenario to my clients. Say I could get you an FDIC-insured CD that guarantees it will pay you 10 percent a year. Would that sound okay?

Of course it would.

There's just one problem. If you're looking for growth, which is really just another term for capital appreciation, then a CD won't work. They don't "grow," they just pay interest. It's all income.

You can see how silly this scenario is.

Of course, this is a purely hypothetical situation. No FDIC-insured[58] CD pays 10 percent interest. If it did, I'd stop writing this book and tell you to throw every last cent you have into it.

I want to make this point crystal clear because it's very important.

When people say they want more "growth" on their money, what they really mean is that they want more return. At the end of the day, most investors don't care whether it comes from the growth or the income, but when they learn that the "I" is a more consistent and secure way of getting return than the "G," they prefer it, especially when they're at or near retirement age and are quite literally battling with time.

It just requires a change of mindset. It requires tweaking your thinking from "growth" to "return." Education helps, but stock market addiction is still hard to break.

OVERCOMING ADDICTION

If you were from my mom's generation, you probably smoked, and all your friends probably smoked as well. You did it for two reasons. The second is that nicotine relaxes you. The first is that it made you look cool.

In some respects, I would have loved to have been an ad man

for cigarette companies in the 1940s and 1950s. I'd be willing to bet it was the easiest job in the world. The stuff practically sold itself.

I probably wouldn't have liked it so much when, in the 1960s onward, research started to come out by the truckload detailing the harmful effects of nicotine on the body and smoke in the lungs. I'm sure I would have hated myself even more in the 1970s and 1980s when those same people I raised on cigarettes started dropping like flies, rivaling the AIDS[59] epidemic.

My mom was one of those people. She started smoking in the early '50s. At first, she did it because it felt good. By the time all the research started coming out two decades later, it didn't matter. She was already hooked. She was addicted. She didn't smoke because it felt good. She did it because she had to.

Here's a couple facts: Between 1960 and 1990, deaths by lung cancer increased by 500 percent. In 1987, lung cancer surpassed breast cancer to become the leading cause of death among U.S. women.[60]

Today, smoking cigarettes is so "un-cool" that many college campuses won't let you do it, and those that do will typically confine you and your cigarette-smoking buddies to a small box on the far south side of the campus.

The way I see it, the cycle moves in three stages:

1. Fun
2. Withdrawal
3. Sobriety

Stage One: In the early days, people smoked because they felt and looked cool.

Stage Two: Decades later, those who still smoked did it because they had to; they were addicted. They didn't smoke to feel good. They smoked so they wouldn't feel bad.

Stage Three: Today, everyone knows cigarettes are bad and most people try to stay away from them.

It's taken a long time for our society and our culture to reach stage three. It's literally taken decades and at least two generations. Now that we're here, there's no going back. The tide has shifted. People have more sense now, and cigarettes will never hold the place in our society that they once did.

I don't know if someday we'll feel the exact same way about the stock market. With cigarettes, we have a symbol, lung cancer, that is embedded in the hearts and minds of people. We can link it to physical death. Financial death is a bit more abstract, but it's all the more threatening.

We know what stage one was—the fun and thrill of the 1980s and 1990s bull market. Stocks were the new game in town, and suddenly, they were the only game in town. People who had once never invested a dime in stocks or stock mutual funds within years were quitting their day jobs to become full-time day traders.

Then came stage two: withdrawal. The markets lost half their value, *twice*. Trillions of dollars in market cap, gone, vanished, poof.

Have we crossed into stage three? Have we woken up? Are we ready to get sober yet?

I'd like to think so, but it doesn't seem like it.

Rather than going into withdrawal, the markets are jacked up on financial leverage like artificially low interest rates, corporate buybacks, and rising debt levels. We're still riding the high of the '80s and '90s like a nicotine addict who, instead of kicking the habit, switched to Nicorette gum, or worse, a vape pen.

The only difference with our culture's addiction to the stock market is that it began much later, and that's why it hasn't yet come full circle.

We had 20 years of an excellent market, followed by 20 years of an uncertain market.

I think another crash might push us over the edge into stage three.

Like with cigarettes, it wasn't until enough people started literally dying when the masses woke up, revolted, and demanded tighter regulations and more transparency on the risks of smoking cigarettes.

What do you think will happen to our society if the market takes another 50 percent dive?

Do you think we'll be just as angry as we were after 2008? Do you think we'll be angrier? How many times will our culture allow this to happen before the people finally say "enough"?

Over the next 10 to 20 years, I suspect we're going to see a radical shift as our generation, the Income Generation, comes to terms with the fact that we've been addicted to a drug that will financially kill us if we don't break the habit.

Eventually it will happen. The party always ends. The gravy train stops rolling.

The bottom line is cigarette smokers had 20–30 years after the "cool" days of the '40s and '50s before large-scale reports surfaced about the medical risks of smoking. Now those reports are taken for granted. As more suffer a financial death from utilizing cancerous financial strategies, talk about investing for the "I" will soon become the norm. When that happens, the Retirement Income Store will be there for them.

CHAPTER 7

Why Doesn't My "Advisor" Talk Like This?

I'M A BLUNT PERSON, I always have been, and frankly, it's one of my greatest assets. When people talk to me, they know right away I'm telling it like it is. I'm a very different kind of financial advisor, because most want you to risk your money to get a return. They'll talk about hypotheticals and dance around the risk so you either ignore it or brush it off. Me, I put the risk front and center. I'm not trying to fool anyone.

Some would say it's a bad sales tactic. After all, greed sells. On the contrary, I've built up one of the largest operations that focuses on income in the country simply because I'm willing to tell my clients the things their typical advisor never will.

First, let's differentiate between the two types of "advisors" you've likely been exposed to.

First is your commission-based salesperson or broker, and the second is a fee-based advisor.

The former is really just that, a salesperson, not really an advisor.

In fact, when a broker helps you invest, they are held to what is known as a "suitability" standard. In other words, they are disallowed from making any recommendations that are blatantly wrong for you and your goals; as long as the recommendation is considered "suitable," then the broker has done his job.

The latter, on the other hand, is considered legally to be an advisor and is held to a "fiduciary" standard. In other words, they must make for you what they believe is the absolute best recommendation for your goals, essentially acting as a fiduciary under the law. In the real world, many "advisors" are licensed to act in both capacities, and often the customer isn't fully aware of the capacity in which they are acting for each transaction.

COMMISSION-BASED BROKERS

Unfortunately, the "suitability standard" is quite broad. For example, taking "income" using the withdrawal method, even if in a fairly high percentage, is typically not considered a violation of the standard, never mind the fact that it means they're depleting your principal. Or consider this: In the eyes of the regulators, it is still considered "suitable" for a 90-year-old with nearly 100 percent of his or her money in stocks or stock funds, or for that same investor holding 30-year bonds that won't mature until long after they're dead. It sounds crazy, but it's true.

In fact, it's worse than that.

Every commission-based broker has to be licensed with a brokerage firm whose job it is to enforce the "suitability" standard. According to the laws of[61] agency, because they are considered acting as an agent of the agency, a broker's primary obligation is to his brokerage firm with whom he has an agency contract, not his customer.

Think for a moment about what that means. Let's say there are two possible recommendations that a broker can make to the client, both of which are considered suitable. One is really good for the client and reasonably good for the firm. The other is really profitable for the firm, even though it is slightly less beneficial to the client. Guess which recommendation, according to the laws of agent/agency, he or she should make?

You guessed it, the one that fulfills his agency's legal requirements. So by their nature, brokers do not have the best interest of their customers in mind, but rather the brokerage firm they're operating under. Sure, there are some brokers that thumb their noses to their supervisor and truly do what they believe is the best thing for their client. But if you are the customer, can you ever be 100 percent sure?

WALL STREET'S CANCER

It gets worse still. I use cancer as a metaphor because it is so fitting. Cancer begins in the human body as one mutated cell. As it spreads, it goes off in any and all directions until it affects the entire body. The same can be said of Wall Street.

Let's say that you are now the CEO of a major brokerage firm with millions of customers and tens of thousands of shareholders to whom you answer. Do you know to whom YOUR fiduciary responsibility would be?

You can probably guess—to your shareholders, not your firm's customers. In fact, that's true with any firm that has shareholders. For example, if you were the CEO of General Motors, your job is to help your company sell more GM automobiles so that it can make as much profit for the shareholders as possible. This means that any marketing information that your research department distributes does not have to be unbiased. Of course, we expect it to be highly favorable toward GM. The dealership owners or sales managers are happy to follow suit and focus on the positives of GM[62] automobiles, as are the salespeople. That is how they make money, by selling more GMs.

So, if it turns out after the fact that a GM vehicle was not ideal for you, then you really can't blame the CEO, the research and marketing department, the sales manager, *or* the salesperson. After all, they were just doing their jobs. The blame is really yours because you went into the wrong dealership.

Now let's be clear: I have a GM car. It's actually my favorite vehicle. But even if it weren't, at the end of the day, it wouldn't be that big of a deal if it was the wrong car for me. I would just live with it until my next vehicle.

The trouble is, this same business model extends to Wall Street where we're not talking about a $20,000 to $30,000 vehicle, but your entire life savings.

Now to be fair, in the brokerage industry, the regulators do really try to correct this by saying that any marketing needs to be "fair and balanced." In other words, it needs to be as close to unbiased as possible. And yes, if you were to read the ENTIRE prospectus (often more than 100 pages), you would get the full story.

But when was the last time that you actually did that?

If you answered "never," then unfortunately you are among the vast majority of investors. Over the years as I have tried to get clients to read the prospectus, they would say, "If I have to read that entire book, and could understand it, then I wouldn't need you." In the real world, much of the broker-customer communication is verbal and unmonitored, and most of what your broker will tell you is whatever sales pitch he picked up from his or her research department.

SO WHAT'S STOPPING THEM FROM GIVING ME WHAT I NEED?

You might be wondering why brokerage firms would not want to promote income-based investing. After all, if there's a market for it, they can probably sell it, right?

They can. But there's a lot more money in stocks. And remember, the company's management has a fiduciary responsibility to its shareholders, not to its customers. If it's more profitable to sell you stocks or related investments, that's what they're going to do.

Consider this: If a brokerage firm sells you a mutual fund or a variable annuity, there is typically 5 percent or so distributed to the firm, the manager, the broker. That's $5,000 on a $100,000 sale.

That's not a bad shake. But they can do even better.

If, instead, they sell you on the concept of individual stocks, the commission would be less per transaction. However, that portfolio of individual stocks needs to be watched a bit more closely and more actively managed.

That means they won't just charge a commission on the one-time sale, but any time they need to buy and sell out of the individual stock, potentially triggering an even bigger revenue stream for the firm than the mutual fund or variable annuity sale over time. Also, the commission on individual securities is flexible and can be negotiated, whereas on the mutual fund or variable annuity it's usually fixed.

Point being, whether it's a mutual fund, variable annuity, or a portfolio of individual stocks, the brokerage firm can make good money. The rewards are potentially higher on a portfolio of stocks, but even on the other securities, they can still make 5 percent.

Now let's look at how that compares to a portfolio of individual bonds.

For brokers, bonds are normally considered a one-and-done type of investment. If you buy a 10-year bond, a broker can only charge you once during the life of that bond. Meaning over a 10-year period, he gets paid only once.

Not only that, but since a bond is *not* considered speculative, he might feel as though he cannot charge as high a commission as a stock. The more speculative the investment, the higher the potential reward, and the higher the potential reward, the higher a broker can often justify in fees. With bonds, we're not going for broke. We're investing for the income. It's a steady Eddie contract designed to get us the exact income we need for our purpose-based goals and nothing more. That's why lower commissions are more or less baked into the cake.

Consider this example. Let's say you go to your typical broker and you want to buy $100,000 worth of bonds. You might think $100,000 is a lot of money. On the sales side, the commission side, it's typically going to translate to about 0.5 percent, just $500.

That's it. One $500 payment for an investment that's going to sit there and do nothing for 5 or 10 years or longer.

As you can imagine, your typical broker can't make a living doing that. He *can* make a living buying and selling stocks. After all, stocks have to be more actively managed. Every time he buys or sells a stock, he might be able to collect a full 1 percent.

What sounds better? Collecting 0.5 percent once every 10 years? Or 5 percent by selling a mutual fund or variable annuity? Or 1 percent once, twice, maybe even three or four times a year by buying and selling stocks?

That's one of the reasons there aren't as many people in this business who specialize in buying bonds and bond-like investments for their clients. There's a much less sinister side to it as well.

Let's face it—the stock market can be much more fun and exciting than bonds. That means that, for many, they provide that path of least resistance in financial sales.

What sounds more attractive to you? With stocks, you have unlimited upside potential. Over the long run, it averages around a 10 percent return, but there have been many years where it has grown by 20 or 30 percent. Then there are bonds and bond-like investments, where the best you will ever do is earn an interest of maybe 5 percent. That's it. So most stock-based businesses already have a much easier time selling you on their model. Then there is our perennial sense of optimism that we have already discussed. Even though you know in your heart that, technically speaking, you can lose 100 percent of your investment, it's easy to ignore the downside and focus on the upside. It is the same temperament that historically has kept stock market investors all in during volatile, zero-growth, and 20-year secular bear-market cycles.

IT'S ALL IN THE NAME

There is a reason that stockbrokers are called stockbrokers, because they typically favor stocks. You show me a real estate broker that says real estate is a bad investment and I will show you a stockbroker who says the same about stocks. It's typically the more aggressively minded individuals that gravitate toward becoming stockbrokers in the first place.

Think about it. If I were your school guidance counselor and you came to me describing yourself as a really, really conservative individual, do you think that I would ever recommend that you start a career as a stockbroker?

Probably not. So why then do many brokers describe themselves as being "conservative"?

Because, in essence, the word "conservative" is just a word. It means different things to different people. I'm sure that you know some extremely conservative people who would never dream of becoming a private pilot because they are just plain too conservative. But, if you were to ask a commercial airline pilot if he is aggressive or conservative, how do you think he'd respond? Conservative. Because he has hundreds of people on board, and because compared to his friend who is an aerobatic stunt pilot and nephew who is a military fighter pilot, he *is* conservative. It's just a word. It means different things to different people.

A commercial airline pilot is still a pilot of a 400-ton airplane. Nothing about flying a steel juggernaut at 30,000 feet is particularly conservative. Put the average person in the cockpit and they'd short-circuit from the pressure and responsibility. So it's very telling, for example, that even commercial pilots become immune to turbulence because they experience it much more often than the rest of us. I believe that, in a similar way, many stockbrokers become immune to risk since virtually every day the market is open, they have some customer who is losing money in some investment. They can become immune to risk and define "conservative" differently from most.

It goes to show you that when stockbrokers call stocks a safe or "conservative" investment, you should take it with a grain of salt.

HOW CANCER SPREADS HORIZONTALLY

So far I've talked about how Wall Street's cancer spreads vertically, from the CEO to the research department to the marketing department to the sales manager and finally to the salesperson, your broker. But cancer in the human body tends to spread in all directions. So how does Wall Street's cancer spread horizontally?

The answer lies within the following question: "Does the media, including television, radio, and print, make most of their money from subscriptions or advertising?"

If you said "advertising," you would be correct.

Again, money talks. Just as a CEO or board of directors is beholden to their shareholders, media organizations are beholden to the advertisers that keep them in business. As you might expect, brokerage firms as well as other financial companies are the primary advertisers in the various forms of financial media.

Imagine that you were the chief marketing officer of a brokerage firm and had to choose on which marketing media firm you would prefer to spend your firm's dollars—one that typically leads investors toward lower profit, more conservative strategies, or the higher profit margin approaches that your firm espouses? The answer is clear. Although the media in theory is unbiased (which we know it's not), media firms still need to stay in business and often have shareholders to which they answer. Their messages are often indirectly affected by their advertisers. They need those advertising dollars from your broker's firm.

Some believe that the "cancer" spreads even further horizontally to the schools that train financial advisors. To stay in business, these schools rely on brokerage firms and the like to encourage their representatives to attend. Would they still do that if what was being taught was contrary to their companies' interests? Moreover, many of these schools were initially funded and continue to be funded by those very same firms.

I saw implications firsthand of how this can create bias.

As you saw in my bio, I have an alphabet soup after my name: David J. Scranton, CLU, ChFC, CFP, CFA, MSFS.

When I was studying for one of these credentials more than two decades ago, I was learning a new "science" of investing, an extension of the Modern Portfolio Theory,[63] which allowed an advisor to mathematically mitigate much of a client's portfolio risk through certain types of diversification, almost like financial alchemy of sorts. I was skeptical because it didn't account for human emotions in investing even though it looked great on paper, until over the last two decades, when it failed to protect investors not once, but twice, in the real world.

Do you want to know what many of these schools are still teaching students today? Yup, you guessed it—the same thing.

Point being, the cancer doesn't just spread vertically through brokerage firms. It spreads horizontally to the media and the schools that educate financial advisors.

FEE-BASED FINANCIAL ADVISORS

Surely, Wall Street's cancer can't spread *everywhere,* you might think. After all, registered investment advisors are at least in theory supposed to act in the best interest of their clients, whereas stockbrokers have a fiduciary duty to their firm. Legally speaking, these advisors act as fiduciaries for their clients.

That puts a lot of people at ease. Many investors feel a greater sense of comfort knowing that they pay a fee instead of a commission for investment advisory services.

The theory is that the advisor earns more money if the client's account grows and less if it shrinks. Also, the advisor earns the same amount of money whether he makes more trades or fewer trades. It doesn't matter if he holds a particular investment for 10 years or changes it several times per year. The fee is the same, whereas with brokers, there's a potential conflict of interest because they make more money the *more* they trade, regardless of the outcome. Alternatively, many investors take solace because, at least in theory, they and their advisor's goals are aligned. They're "sitting on the same side of the table," so to speak. While all this is true, most still don't espouse the principles in this book.

I cannot answer the "why" for every investment advisor in America because I don't know every single one of them. I'm also not a mind reader. And this is where Wall Street's cancer can afflict not just brokers, but investment advisors alike.

CANCER SPREADS EVERYWHERE

Like brokers, financial advisors realize that, the riskier the portfolio, the more active management is required. Many feel that more active management helps them justify a higher fee. Most advisors charge fees in excess of 1 percent of the assets being managed.

So let's say that your advisor had you invested in an extremely conservative portfolio of nicely laddered government bonds, so there was no default risk and no active management required. Tell me, how long would you want to pay a 1 percent fee to that advisor before you said, "Enough?" For sure, this is an extreme example, but do you get my point? The fee may not be so bad when double-digit returns are possible and at stake, but if your interest payment is only 3 percent, and the advisor takes 1 of that 3 percent, you're only netting 2 percent. Your advisor is earning one-half as much as you. Of course, most advisors don't have their clients heavily invested in bonds because they themselves aren't familiar with them. They put them in stocks because that's the business they know. Many of these guys were stockbrokers before they became advisors.

True to the point, most fee-based accounts managed by investment advisors that I stumble across seem to have at least 50–70 percent invested in stocks or stock mutual funds, even for retirees or those nearing retirement. I am always amazed, wondering just how this one-size-fits-all solution can be considered to have fulfilled one's fiduciary duty. Hopefully, if you got this far in this book, you're wondering the same.

Basic Modern Portfolio Theory, the "alchemy" I described before, is considered by many to still be the "gold standard" today. It attempts to evaluate return versus volatility risk for all the different stocks and bonds or combinations. Combined with "Monte Carlo" math (discussed in Chapter 3), it creates something called the "efficient frontier,"[64] which takes all the various stock/bond combinations to find the one that, in theory, results in the most return for the risk taken. According to that model, the "efficient frontier" only includes portfolios that have 40 percent or more in stocks or stock funds. Meaning no portfolios with less than 40 percent in stocks or stock funds are considered "efficient," regardless of income needs.

This may work in a theoretical world, where people have an indefinite period for which they can hold their investments, but in the real world, when they retire and need income, it doesn't. Some investors who want more income might need to reduce their stock exposure well below 40 percent to generate it. The problem is that the Modern Portfolio Theory bases all its returns on total return, with absolutely no differentiation between income and growth. In other words, it assumes that people get their cash flow utilizing the withdrawal method, not the income method.

So as an advisor, you might think that with more than 50 percent in the stock market:

1. Clients might be willing to pay you higher management fees.
2. You have less regulatory and legal risk adhering to the "Gold Standard" of the investment markets.
3. You have a sexier, more exciting business model.
4. You can use mutual funds or ETFs and simplify your business.

It's a home run for you; it could be a strikeout for some of your clients.

LAZINESS, PURE AND SIMPLE

Let's admit it together—human beings tend to be inherently lazy. We're the smartest creatures in the animal kingdom, and as such, we know how to work smarter, not harder, so we can relax more. We tend to take the path of least resistance whenever possible. Since advisors are human beings, it should be no surprise that this tendency affects them also.

This may seem hard to believe, but today most investment advisors don't really manage money at all. Some, vis-à-vis my fourth bullet point above, utilize mutual funds or ETFs. These funds have fund managers who actually do the money management within each fund so your advisor doesn't have to. All your advisor has to do is choose the right combination of funds and rebalance them occasionally, leaving a lot of leftover time to focus on growing his or her business.

Here's the problem with that. In the case of mutual funds especially, there tends to be higher fees, and I don't mean the fee you are paying your advisor; I am referring to the embedded fees inside the mutual fund. The fees that you forget about because they are not readily visible unless you look on page 87 of the prospectus.

Imagine if your auto mechanic couldn't fix your car, so he charged you a referral fee to send you to the proper mechanic whom you would then have to pay a separate fee to repair your vehicle. That's two sets of fees for one job. My friend Greg (the chicken and egg guy) says advisors have essentially gotten so lazy that all they want to do is check off a box on an application, which is all it really takes for one to invest your dollars in a mutual fund. Then they try to convince you that doing nothing is okay. He calls it "The Disease of Ease."[65]

Granted, there are some advisors who include individual stocks in client portfolios, but many of them still don't really do any money management. Often, they have anywhere from five to ten different preset portfolios that they utilize. For example, they might have one that has 100 percent stock, another that has 80 percent stocks and 20 percent bonds, one that is 60/40 or 40/60, and so on. They normally ask you to complete a "risk tolerance questionnaire." Then they input your answers into a computer algorithm, which then determines the portfolio that best fits you. Done. Simple, painless; your money gets invested in the pool and your advisor is off to search for his next client. The only problem is that the portfolio was probably chosen based on the Modern Portfolio Theory and other factors, none of which differentiates between the "Income" and the "Growth." Again, "The Disease of Ease."

STOCK MARKET CHEERLEADERS

Cheerleaders have one job, to cheer. It doesn't matter if their team is winning or losing. They cheer regardless because that is what cheerleaders do.

The same is true for most brokers and advisors. They're stock market cheerleaders.

When are you more excited to invest money in the market? Is it when markets are climbing and everyone is optimistic or when markets are declining and pessimism abounds? The answer is obvious—optimism is contagious. The stock market cheerleaders know this. In many ways, they are in the business of selling optimism. This might explain why, when markets are climbing, you are told that it is a good time to invest, but when markets are down you are told that it is a great chance to buy low. No matter the situation, they want you to think it's always a great time to buy.

Now be honest with yourself. When you read Chapter 4 about these long-term secular stock market cycles, wasn't it the first time that you've heard these cycles discussed so succinctly? How predictable and repeatable they seem to have been throughout history? Whenever I present that historical data, I typically hear, "So shouldn't we just get out of the market for those twenty years or so of bear-market cycles?" Brokers and advisors know that wouldn't be good for their business.

Several years ago, I was mentoring the daughter of a friend. She worked with us as an intern over the summer. I had a television interview at the New York Stock Exchange[66] and thought that it might be a good experience for her if she tagged along. I finished my interview and only a few minutes remained until the closing bell (4:00 p.m. EST) so I thought we'd stick around. Sure enough, at 4:00 p.m. sharp, the bell rang and EVERYONE on the balcony started to applaud and cheer. My intern looked at me and proclaimed, "Mr. Scranton, there they are, the stock market cheerleaders you always talk about."

"Yes," I said, "easy to spot applauding in large groups but not so easy one-on-one in their offices. Notice, they are not wearing their cheerleader uniforms."

THE INFORMATION'S GOT TO COME FROM SOMEWHERE

Even totally "independent" brokers and advisors fall into this trap.

Let's say, for example, that a broker is registered with a smaller independent family-owned brokerage firm (not one of the big brokerage houses who have to answer to shareholders).

That smaller firm probably cannot afford to have its own research department. That broker is then expected to do his own research.

The only problem is that he is unlikely to have enough time available to do that. Between prospecting for new clients, servicing existing clients, maybe doing paperwork, keeping up with compliance requirements, actually meeting with prospects or clients, and managing his office, research often falls to the bottom of the list. Even if that broker has two or three full-time employees, that is a lot to ask.

So most get their research by purchasing it from an outside source. Some are "lucky" enough that their firms actually pay for it. But where do you think that research typically comes from in the first place?

Bingo.

The original source of most of this information is tied directly or indirectly to the larger brokerage firms, those who *do* have to answer to shareholders.

So what about independent investment advisors? After all, they are fiduciaries. True, except that they have the same time limitations as those with an independent brokerage house, maybe worse. Most attempt to do some research on their own but ultimately need the help of an outside source, similar to those that are available to brokers.

In other words, they both fall into the same trap.

Remember, brokers and advisors are human beings, susceptible to all the same emotional factors affecting those of you who manage your own investments. Optimism, check. Recency bias, check.[67] A stock market paradigm if he or she got into the industry between 1980–2000, 2003–2007, or after 2009, check. Finally, susceptible to addictions where the longer the addiction, the more difficult the recovery, check.

Unless they struggle with an affliction such as Asperger's, humans make decisions emotionally first, and only then do we attempt to justify them logically. It is simply how 99 percent of all humans are wired, regardless of professional training.

DON'T GET SWEPT UP BY THE HERD

Like sheep, many "advisors" today think there is no other way. They invest for growth because it's the only thing they've been taught, and, ultimately, they follow the herd over a cliff.

That may not be fair to sheep. Sheep get a bad reputation for being the stupidest animals on earth. The reality is that sheep are surprisingly intelligent. They have long memories, they remember faces, and they form bonds with their friends and masters. They also feel sadness when one of their own gets sent to the slaughter.

But herd mentality is very real. It's been studied in both humans and animals. We're all programmed, on some level, to do what everyone around us is doing, even if it flies in the face of common sense and puts us in grave danger.

For decades, the herd rode the stock market to great riches. It was all advisors knew. Then when the party ended, they stayed in the market, because it was still all they knew.

Essentially, they have forgotten that return, your *total* return, is made up of two components, growth *and* income.

Written out, it looks like this:

$$TR = G + I$$

Write that down. Put it on a small piece of paper. Stick it in your wallet and commit it to memory. *Total return equals growth plus income.*

It may sound like a simple formula, but the majority of investors, brokers, and advisors alike have forgotten this simple equation after years and years of programming to feel differently. We've been taught that the only way to make return is through the "G," through growth.

Sure, for most of the last 10 years, the "G" has been great. We just saw one of the greatest bull markets in history, where the average stock quadrupled in price from its 2009 lows.

But let me ask you: Has your money quadrupled since 2009?

Probably not. Otherwise, you wouldn't be reading this book, and I wouldn't be writing it.

So yes, for the last decade there's been a lot of the "G" to go around, *if* you timed the market perfectly and picked the best stocks, which no one does, and which no one can do consistently.

CHAPTER 8

Have You Outgrown Your Current Advisor?

LOVED MY DOCTOR GROWING up. Most children hate going to the doctor. For most parents it's like herding cats, or, God forbid, trying to give one a pill.

Not me. I loved my pediatricians. In fact, everyone loved them. Dr. Becker and Dr. Glass were the best of the best. I loved them so much that by the time I was 20, *I was still going to them.*

It must have been quite a sight. There I was, a 20-year-old bodybuilder, six feet tall, 270 pounds, surrounded by a bunch of children and still going to see my pediatrician. I didn't mind it so much. My doctors were great. As the old saying goes—if it ain't broke, don't fix it.

The fact is, I had outgrown them, and I didn't want to accept it. So eventually, the doctors called me up one day and broke the news. They told me I had to select a primary care doctor. An *adult* primary care doctor.

I didn't like it at first. No one likes change when it's forced on them. But in time, I came to like my new doctor just fine.

Now, I share this rather silly and frankly embarrassing story with you to illustrate a point. When it comes to our finances, there are people who specialize in the growth or the accumulation phase of our wealth, just as there are pediatricians who specialize in treating growing children. It's a mistake to assume that the same financial doctor who helped you grow your investments is the same one who can help you protect them during your income years. It's as silly as going to a pediatrician until you're 20 years old.

My doctor today, Dr. Gaudio, is just as good as the doctors I had when I was little. I love going to see him. But one of these days, I'm going to outgrow him, too. Eventually my health will start to decline, and I'll have to seek out a doctor who specializes in geriatric medicine.

I won't like it. I probably won't make the choice of my own volition. One of these days, Dr. Gaudio is going to call me into his office and tell it to me straight. *Dave, it's time to get a new doctor.*

It's the same with money; except you'll never find an advisor who will tell you to go somewhere else (unless you put your foot down that you're only interested in individually managed bonds and bond-like instruments). There are financial advisors who specialize in the stock market, and there are advisors who specialize in the market for bonds and similar types of investments, just as there are doctors who treat adults, and those who treat the elderly. What is right for one is not necessarily right for the other.

The fact is, unless you're in Florida, there are a LOT more doctors who treat regular-aged adults than there are those who treat senior citizens, and of those doctors, there are only a few good ones.

They are out there—and finding the right one can literally mean the difference between life and death.

It's the same with finding the bond advisor. There are a lot of stock advisors out there. There are even fewer bond advisors, and of the ones available, there are only some who know how to manage a portfolio of individual bonds and bond-like investments the Dave Scranton way.

I say this as a person who has spent the last 20 years of my career specializing in this smaller niche of the market, as well as building up a national network of advisors who do the same.

It's as simple as this—the advisor you may have worked with for the past 20 years helping you grow your assets is *not* the advisor you want to help you *protect* your assets, and he's probably not the best one to help you generate your "I."

MARK THIS PAGE

If you take nothing else from this book, I want you to really highlight this next section. I'm serious. Get a *Post-It note*. Earmark the page. Do something so you don't forget this.

As discussed in Chapter 7, it's true that a broker can't make a living buying $100,000 worth of individual bonds and bond-like investments for his clients. It's too much work for most because they can only charge a very small fee, and only do it once for the life of the bond. But $100,000 is still a lot of money. Your advisor still wants to have it under his management. So, rather than buy a basket of individual bonds, he's going to put you in something called a "bond mutual fund."

Sounds okay, right? Everyone loves mutual funds, and we know bonds are more conservative investments.

Most investors will be okay with this. In fact, this is what most likely happens the majority of the time when an investor approaches a financial advisor and says they want to put their money in bonds.

There's just one problem: It's not a bond. It's a bond *mutual fund*.[68]

So when your typical investor hears the term "bond mutual fund," it checks off two boxes in his head.

1. He knows he needs bonds.
2. He knows he likes mutual funds.

Here's what he doesn't know: A bond mutual fund gives you neither of the two guarantees that make a diversified portfolio of individual bonds attractive, but contains all the risks of mutual funds. In fact, if you were to study for the examination to become an investment advisor, the textbook would say that a bond fund is really not a bond at all; it is the stock of a company that owns bonds. It even sounds riskier.

This is one of my biggest challenges as a financial advisor. As a population, we have mutual fund addiction. When I ask people which instrument they think would be safer, a bond or a bond mutual fund, they're going to tell me the latter because that's what they were taught.

But it's wrong.

INVESTMENT BY CONTRACT

Here's the difference between buying a stock and buying a bond: When you buy a stock, you cross your fingers and you hope it goes up. At the end of the day, it's pure speculation. You're betting on the company and the management team in place.

So back to our friend, the "bond mutual fund."[69] Remember those two guarantees we mentioned earlier in the book—a guaranteed amount of interest for the life of the bond and guaranteed repayment of principal at maturity? Great. Now forget them. Pretend they never existed. That, in short, is your bond fund.

A bond fund is simply a regular ol' mutual fund, except instead of investing in stocks, it pools its money in bonds. Many investment advisors consider it a simpler way of investing in bonds. You want to avoid those investment advisors, because they don't know what they're talking about.

FIXED INCOME INVESTING			
MUTUAL FUNDS		INDIVIDUAL BONDS	
Fixed Income	No	Permanent Income	Yes
Definite Maturity	No	Definite Maturity	Yes
Return of Principal	No	Return of Principal	Yes
Management Fees	Yes	Management Fees	No
Know What You Own	No	Know What You Own	Yes

Table B

That's because, unlike bonds, when you buy into a bond mutual fund, there's no contract. With a bond, you know what you get, what you get back, and when you get it. If it's a 2-year bond, you get your money back in two years. If it's a 30-year bond, you get it back in 30.

The payments are fixed.

With a bond mutual fund, everything is *variable*.

THE DISEASE OF EASE

The solution, of course, is just to buy a portfolio of *actual* bonds—except, it's not that easy.

As I explained, there's less money in it for a broker and possibly the advisor. Since money talks, and there's not a lot of money in bonds as far as advisors are concerned, there is a limited pool of experienced advisors who specialize in this field to choose from, at least compared to the wide pool of advisors who specialize in stocks. That means fewer of those with experience or with an already established clientele will be willing to take you on as a client. Worse, the ones who will take you on as a client might not know what they're doing, either.

Consider it like this: Have you ever met someone who is both an orthopedic surgeon and a chiropractor? Probably not. They're usually either one or the other. That's because each field requires a high degree of specialization, education, and experience. Anyone who's smart knows they shouldn't go to an orthopedic surgeon when what they really need is a chiropractor, and vice versa.

It's the same in the financial industry. Advisors typically specialize in either the stock market or the bond market. Very few specialize in both, and the ones who do probably aren't a renowned specialist in either.

I, for one, would be a terrible advisor to a 30-year-old client with a $200,000 portfolio. That client doesn't want 5 and 6 percent investing for the "I." He wants 8 to 10 percent investing for the "G." Quite frankly, if he wants that, he needs to invest in stocks. I haven't focused on growth-based strategies in 20 years. My specialization since 1999 has been income, so I'm not his guy.

If you're 50 years old or older—in other words, at or near retirement age—I'm your guy, and if I'm not your guy for geographical reasons, I can put you in touch with someone who is your guy, because there aren't that many of us out there, at least compared to your typical investment advisor.

You have to remember that, for most investment advisors, their specialization—i.e., the stuff they *actually* know—is the stock market, not the bond market.

So let me ask you this: If you need a knee replacement, and you know a chiropractor who is also an orthopedic surgeon and has successfully performed 10 knee replacements to date, will you let him operate on you?

Maybe, if the price is right and he has another expert in the room who knows what he's doing. You also might have a *really* good lawyer who can make that kind of fiasco waiting to happen worth your while.

Otherwise, you likely wouldn't let him perform his eleventh surgery on you.

While he may know how to perform the surgery, he's *never* going to be as good as the full-time orthopedic surgeon who has performed over 1,000 of these surgeries successfully with minimal marks on his otherwise seamless record. Chances are, if that chiropractor was good enough at his chiropractic work, he wouldn't have needed to double up. Both are very specialized fields that require years of training and experience.

So, too, for financial advisors, you can't expect an advisor who has spent his entire life dealing with stocks to know what he's doing when he tries to apply his same skills to the bond market. Even he understands this, though he likely won't admit as much.

The problem is that investing in bonds *the right way* requires a great deal of skill, experience, and know-how.

Do you think those advisors learned any of that skill and know-how, as it pertains to the bond market, during the 1980s and 1990s when stocks were the only game in town? Not hardly, and that's why they buy bond mutual funds instead of a diversified portfolio of individual bonds.

They wouldn't even know where to start.

You might think it's as easy as going to the U.S. Treasury and buying a 10-Year bond that pays a fixed rate of interest. Except Treasuries aren't what they used to be. Back in the early '90s, you could still get 8 percent on a 10-Year Treasury. Today, in the middle of 2019, the most you'll get is a little over 2 percent, and unless you've got millions of dollars to play with, that two to three percent isn't going to cut it.

That's okay; there are plenty of investments out there that will pay you twice that much without risking your money in stocks.

However, if your advisor has been playing with stocks his whole life, it's probably safe to say he has no idea where to find them or how to negotiate a good price, let alone how to do good by his clients, including you.

That's why your typical advisor will put you in bond mutual funds when you say you want to shed some of the risk from your portfolio. He doesn't know how to do anything else.

It's the "Disease of Ease" and it's a disease that's spread throughout the entire financial industry. It looks pretty plain and simple on the one hand. They can't get the job done right. But on the other hand, the Securities and Exchange Commission (SEC)[70] won't come knocking on their door for putting their clients in bond funds, either.

Now you might wonder if good fixed-income investments are out there, and your advisor who is a fiduciary has to act in your best interest, how can they possibly get credit for merely putting their clients in bond funds that have none of the benefits of actual bonds?

It's a good question. The answer is simply because their clients don't know the difference (and because the advisors themselves may not know the difference). From a regulator's standpoint, interest rates in general had been declining from 1981–2014, providing bond mutual funds with a tailwind for a very long time. When things are going up, clients are happy even if they don't completely understand why. All that changed around 2015 when interest rates started to climb due to the Fed's reversal of quantitative easing and other factors. The tailwind is turning into a headwind and clients are beginning to notice the effect on bond funds. Eventually, regulators will take notice.

Fortunately, you can use this knowledge to arm yourself.

WHAT SEPARATES US FROM EVERYONE ELSE

As mentioned, most advisors know stocks and that's it. Of the ones who will put your money in bonds, most will use bond funds, which really aren't bonds but more like the stock of a company that owns them. It gets you none of the benefits or guarantees that come with owning bonds while subjecting you to most of the same risks of owning stocks.

So, what *should* you look for when you're searching for a good bond advisor?

There are five things a good bond advisor must do in order to manage a portfolio effectively. By effectively, I mean they must know how to protect your wealth through a diversified portfolio of individually managed bonds that can generates roughly 5 percent in income every year so you never have to withdraw from your principal if you don't want to. Every advisor we have listed on the Retirement Income Store website must meet the following five criteria.

NUMBER 1

As you can probably guess by now, we don't use bond funds. We invest in individual bonds and bond-like investments. If an advisor can't get this first step right, then he or she doesn't really specialize in the "I." Period. This one criterion alone separates us from more than 90 percent of the advisory community out there. But we don't stop there, not even close.

NUMBER 2

Second, we look beyond the ratings agencies and examine the actual financials of the companies we are considering.

As shocking as it may seem, many advisors don't do this.

It's baffling considering the hard lesson learned in 2007 and 2008 that you cannot trust the ratings agencies to be honest with their credit-worthy assessments. After all, they had issued countless AAA ratings on the very mortgage bonds that brought down the economy. If one wouldn't give the rating desired to the company in question, the bond issuer would simply go down the street to the other and get it. Because these agencies are "for profit" businesses, they straddle a very fine line.

The result? You tend to FEEL safe because the ratings agencies issued a AAA rating, even if you are not. If you've ever seen the movie *The Big Short*, you know how this played out. There's this prescient moment in the movie when the protagonists talk it out with a female ratings agent. They ask, "Why would you give these bonds such a high rating if you knew the underlying assets were junk?" Her response: "If we didn't, the guys next door would."

Again, money talks. That's why we don't just look at a bond's rating. Sure, a AAA rating is great, but it's not enough. That's why we have to dig into the security's actual financial ratios for us to feel secure with the investment. It's like the old parable: You can have the sturdiest, most immaculate home in the world, but if it's resting on a bed of sand, it's no good. It has to be built on a firm foundation.

NUMBER 3

This is a big one. Third, we use limit orders.

Most financial advisors who do the first two steps will miss this one. They simply buy investments at whatever price the market is offering that day. They are in too much of a hurry to invest your money so they often overpay for it.

Limit orders are important for this very reason—you never want to overpay for your investments.

By placing a limit order at a desired price level, we are simply waiting for an investment to drop to that level. When it does, the buy order triggers automatically without the potential for human error.

This can take days, sometimes weeks, but that's okay. You want to get the right price. It's one thing to do that with stocks, which can offer growth. By saving 1 or 2 percent, you make up that 1 or 2 percent when you eventually sell your stock. But it only happens once.

The difference with fixed income investments is that you have to remember the interest or divident is fixed. That means that by paying less, you can buy more; therefore, you will earn more interest each and every year that you hold the security. And not just once, like stocks, but every year. So, limit orders are important with stocks, but they are essential with securities. You have to be very strategic when you're tackling the fixed income market.

NUMBER 4

Fourth, we use Bloomberg technology. It's not cheap, but again, we're trying to get the best deal for our clients, which is why a good advisor must spend the time and resources to search for the best buying opportunities. We want to get the highest quality bonds with the highest potential yield.

The beauty of Bloomberg Terminals,[71] named after, of course, Michael Bloomberg himself—is that they give a bond manager a lot of transparency in the bond market specifically. This is helpful because the bond market, although bigger than the stock market, is less liquid than the stock market.

If you want to buy Apple stock, for example, you can be reasonably assured that you can get it for about the same price it was trading for five seconds ago, because it has a pretty large trading volume. The seller gets the money from the buyer and the commission is visible to both parties. Most large-cap stocks[72] are like this. They're that liquid and that transparent. That's because there are plenty of shares available at all times.

The bond market is different. For a given bond issue, there might be only a handful or less of real potential sellers in any particular moment, not millions of shares as is often the case with stocks. Sometimes, there are no particular sellers at all in a given day or possibly several days for that matter.

That's why I have several analysts that sit in front of a Bloomberg Terminal every hour the market is open so they can pounce on these opportunities.

That brings us to the second part of this step.

We don't just have analysts sitting in front of a computer watching the market go by. When a bond issue goes up for sale, we often go directly to the seller to negotiate a fair price for our clients.

You see, when a bond issue is for sale, they might "advertise" an asking price. Potential buyers can then bid on the bond similar to an auction. Traditionally, this is done through a clearing house, which is a company that has a seat on an exchange. There's a bid, there's an ask, and then there's a negotiating until the seller finds the price he wants.

The clearing house in the middle is facilitating a settlement price on behalf of both parties. In exchange for this service, it is "marking up" the price of the bond.

When the transaction is complete, most sellers don't know what the buyer paid and most buyers don't know what the seller received. One seller might be willing to sell the same bond for a lower price than the buyer is willing to pay. In this case, the middleman gets a windfall. In the stock market, on the other hand, shares are traded through an exchange so that every share of a particular stock or security trading at the same time trades for pretty close to the same price so the buyer and the seller get to keep the windfall for themselves. Also, the commission is often much smaller and completely transparent to both parties, that's the difference.

Bloomberg technology tells us who is looking to sell a certain type of bond that we want to buy for our clients. It tells us the asking price without any middleman's markup. That's what is key.

With that information in hand, we can go directly to the seller and negotiate a fair price. We can negotiate with different sellers at the same time to see who will give us the best price.

The reality is that, with this technology, we make bond purchases through our clearing house less than 10 percent of the time. And 90 percent of our bond trades happen as a direct result of using the technology to identify sellers and negotiate a fair price with them directly and a better price than we can typically get through the middleman.

Guess what happens when we wish to sell a particular holding. The same thing happens all over again, this time in reverse. The technology gives us the transparency we need to negotiate the highest price we can.

Most advisors won't do this. In fact, most can't. They don't have the resources or the personnel. Instead, they'll go straight to their clearing house and pay whatever price is on offer, including the middleman's markup. That's why it's important to have an advisor with the right infrastructure in place.

These may seem like small details, and some of them are, but for our clients it can mean the difference of thousands of dollars per year in extra income. When it comes to bonds, *every decimal point counts*. If we can get an extra 0.001 percent, we'll do it. Even if it's just a difference of a few hundred dollars, we go the extra mile, because it's our job. It's our mission to do right by our clients. And more importantly, it's just the right thing to do, period.

NUMBER 5

Fifth and final, we actively manage our portfolios.

This is what truly separates us from other advisors.

Between 1981 and 2014, interest rates were in a loosening cycle. That is, they were in an overall declining trend.

Generally speaking, as interest rates fall, bond prices tend to go up. This meant that, for more than 30 years, bonds and bond-like investments essentially had a tailwind. One could buy a bond and hold onto it knowing the price would more likely go up than down.

However, interest rates started rising after 2014. In an interest rate tightening cycle, one in which interest rates are rising, that tailwind turns into a headwind. It requires active management.

In this environment, the concept of buy low and sell high may be simple but it's not easy. It takes experience and know-how. Our advantage here is that we are one of the few willing to carry the fixed-income cross and, quite frankly, I'm one of the few people in the business who has been carrying it for the last 20 years. I know how this market works.

The stock market is said to be very "efficient," meaning that information today about any particular stock, including current pricing, is immediately available to anyone with a computer.

This means that it is really difficult for anyone to have a trading advantage over another in the stock market. It's become more difficult for an investor to out-perform the market than ever before. Liquidity and transparency lead to efficiency.

In the bond market, however, there's less liquidity. Less liquidity means less efficiency. This reduced efficiency creates what I refer to as dislocations in the bond market. These dislocations often provide for swap opportunities within our portfolios.

Let's say I own a block of a certain type of corporate bonds that pays a 5 percent yield. In theory, all similar bonds should go for the same price and offer the same yield, assuming the same ratings, same industry, same maturity, and so on.

But sometimes dislocations occur, meaning any one of these variables might be different for similar bonds. So, whereas every share of Apple trades for the same price, in the bond market, it's a little trickier.

For example, assume that some insurance company, for some reason, is trying to sell a big block of one of those bonds. To do so, it may have to "advertise" a slightly lower ask price. This means a slightly higher yield, perhaps 5.1 or 5.2 percent. That gives us an opportunity to sell the bonds we own that pay 5 percent, and buy the ones paying a slightly higher return at 5.1 or 5.2 percent. That's a difference that can add up and one of the many reasons I have my portfolio managers keep their eyes peeled for these opportunities.

The thing is, these dislocations may not happen often, but when they do, they may just last for a few hours, sometimes not even that. That's why we actively manage our portfolios to stay on top of any swap opportunities. That's why we have CFAs and other analysts who sit in front of a Bloomberg Terminal all day and do just that.

Most financial advisors can't afford to hire an analyst, let alone a CFA or team of CFAs, and they certainly don't have the time to sit in front of the terminal themselves. They have to see clients. So as a result, they miss the opportunity.

FOUR TYPES OF SWAPS

There are four types of swaps we look out for. I don't want to get too deep into the weeds here, but the first two swaps are designed to increase our return, and they are offensive measures. These are "pay me now" and "pay me later." The last two are more defensive. These are "cover my assets I" and "cover my assets II." And yes, I named them to be a bit tongue in cheek.

1. **Pay me now.** That's when we sell out of a block of bonds and bond-like instruments to buy different bonds and bond-like instruments with a better current yield—in other words, more interest today.
2. **Pay me later.** This is where we increase the yield to maturity. Unlike current yield, yield to maturity also accounts for any gain or loss between the purchase price and the face amount that will contractually be repaid at maturity. In other words, it represents the actual economic internal rate of return if held to maturity.
3. **Cover my assets I.** This swap decreases duration; in other words, it reduces our interest rate risk. Different bonds and bond-like instruments have different levels of susceptibility to changes in interest rates.

4. **Cover my assets II**. In this one, we reduce our credit risk. Credit risk refers to the chance that the issuer of the bond will default on its debt obligations. When we get the chance to protect our clients, we take it.

That's it. Four types of swaps; pay me now, pay me later, cover my assets I, and cover my assets II; and our five rules for investing in bonds, which are:

1. Buy actual bonds and not bond funds.
2. Look beyond the ratings agencies.
3. Don't buy at the market; use limit orders instead.
4. Have a CFA utilize a Bloomberg Terminal to negotiate better prices instead of buying bonds through your clearing house; and
5. Actually manage the portfolio as a financial advisor is supposed to do.

That's what makes our approach so effective and so different. It's possible that you'll never find a stock advisor who knows how to do this, and you'll be hard pressed to find a bond advisor outside our network who can, either.

It isn't easy. It takes work. I compare it to climbing a rope in high school gym class. When you climb a rope, you get a few pulls in, then you wrap your feet around the rope so you don't slide back down. Then you rest. When you've caught your breath, you get a few more pulls in, then you wrap your feet and rest again. Pull, wrap, rest. That's what fixed-income investing is like. You get spurts of swap opportunities and they slow down. The opportunities dry up. So you rest. Knowing that individual bonds are a contract with guaranteed terms is like wrapping your feet so you can't slide back down.

Or, think of it like having a sailboat that only does six knots maximum speed, and that's if the wind cooperates. Sometimes it's a lot slower. So, let's say that one day you have no wind at all. If the current happens to be pushing you toward your destination, no problem. But what if the current is moving against you? What do you do? Do you let it push you back? No. You drop anchor. You wait for the current to pass. And we can do that because we're buying individual bonds; it is like dropping the anchor. Worst-case scenario, we hold our bonds to maturity and continue collecting the income on those investments. You drop anchor, you lock your legs, and you wait for the next opportunity.

Let me be real with you. Even affluent investors have a hard time finding a fixed-income manager who is willing, or even knows how to do, what we do.

It's hard. It's really hard. It takes sacrifice. That's why I often refer to it as bearing the cross. There's not as much money in it for us, and frankly it's a lot more difficult. It's burdensome. It requires a mind toward doing what's right.

It would be a lot more profitable for me to take the easy road and use the old stock market model or, even better, just use bond funds. But remember, since the hyperinflation of the 1970s, interest rates had been falling. They'd been falling all the way through to the financial crisis when the Federal Reserve ultimately lowered overnight interest rates to zero percent and drove down long-term rates with quantitative easing. Bonds had a massive tailwind at their back, driving prices up. For more than 30 years, you could have just bought and held onto bonds knowing that interest rates were going down. When interest rates drop, bond prices tend to go up.

So when Janet Yellen announced in 2013 that the Fed was going to begin *raising* interest rates and reverse QE, it marked a shift for income-seeking investors. And it marked a shift in my business and my mission.

Now, with interest rates on the rise, that tailwind was about to turn into a headwind. We had to be more strategic. We had to actively manage these bonds and bond-like investments the way some advisors actively manage a portfolio of stocks. The only other option was to actively manage these portfolios as a broker, charging a half percent every time. I might actually make more money, except it wouldn't make sense for our clients. They would go broke with fees. That's why I switched toward the investment advisory model so I could actively manage these portfolios in a way that's cost effective for my clients. The goal is to get THEM 5 percent a year. It's not so Mr. Advisor can get rich.

CHAPTER 9

Our Big Fat Hairy Audacious Goal

I MENTIONED THIS BRIEFLY IN the first chapter, but prior to entering college, I had a conversation with my high school guidance counselor about a serious concern of mine. I learned pretty early on in high school that I hated writing, and anytime a teacher assigned an essay, whether it was two paragraphs or ten pages, the result was the same—I'd put it off until the last minute because I had zero interest in doing it. So, I asked my guidance counselor what major I could select in college that all but guaranteed I would never have to write a single essay. And that's the story of how I came to be a math major.

It's taken me about six months to put this book together, and it's been a long, arduous six months. I feel the same way about writing in my 50s as I did as a teenager. But the past six months have nothing on the past 20 years I've spent fighting tooth and nail against Wall Street and the financial establishment to try to bring some financial sanity to this great country.

When I made the leap into the world of investing for income in 1999, lots of people thought I was crazy. Why would I bother with anything else when stocks were so hot? The answer soon became clear. The market crashed. And in a financially coherent world, you might think or at least hope that would be the end of the story. You would think that people would have wised up. When the market crashed in 2000 and my clients were safe, I certainly felt like I had won some all-important debate and I could put the issue to rest. But I never imagined just how deeply entrenched the idea of getting rich in the stock market had become in our culture.

I don't delude myself for a moment, and I don't think anyone does, that *everyone* gets to be rich. We all get our shot, and some make it, and some don't, and that's okay. You don't have to be rich to lead a happy life. Gallup reported in 2011[73] that our happiness peaks at $75,000 in annual income, and that any amount over that doesn't really lead to a significant improvement in our overall quality of life.

So I don't think for a moment that everyone gets to be rich or that they need to, but I do believe that those who work hard should be able to afford a decent life for themselves. And I believe that if you work hard your entire life, you shouldn't have to work as hard in retirement.

That's why I created The Retirement Income Store. At the end of the day, retirees need income, not growth, and if they keep relying on growth to get their investment returns, that money won't be there when the market takes another dive, and that's when they'll need it most. We tend to think that the older we get, the less money we need, but the opposite is really the case. The more you age, the more money you need. Inflation, growing healthcare costs, and growing life spans are just three reasons why. There are psychological reasons, too. No one wants to watch their precious nest egg dwindle the older and more frail they get. Investing for income is all about keeping your security blanket so you can live the lifestyle you want without having to worry about it.

At the Retirement Income Store, we're carrying the mantle of reasonable returns in the form of income with less risk because that's what a growing number of retirees and near-retirees actually need.

We spend nearly 20 years in school learning to become productive members of society. We spend 40 years working and actually being those productive members. With that sort of contract, it sounds reasonable that we should get to retire for the last 20 years, share our wisdom with the younger generation, and allow them to be the stewards of the world we left for them.

Unfortunately, we don't live in a perfect society. We live in one run by humans, and humans are flawed by nature.

It is unfathomable to think about the extent our world has developed in recent history. If you think of the last 2,000 years of global GDP,[74] it looks like this.

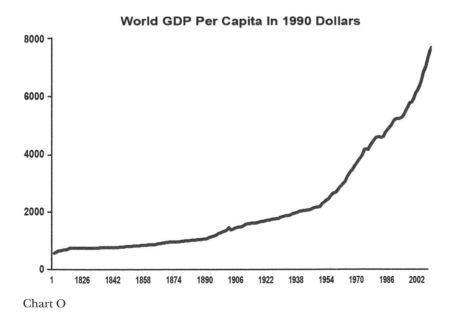

Chart O

Society has developed so rapidly that we're still working out the kinks. We have so much greed in the world because so much wealth happened so quickly. There's so much wealth available in the world that wasn't available even 100 years ago that it's driven people to be insatiable with their thirst for money.

That's why we're so addicted to stocks. In our culture, stocks represent the greatest potential for a person who comes from nothing to rise to the highest echelons of society. Yes, we can start businesses. We can compete in the economy. But with stocks, you have the chance to buy something and watch it multiply 10-, 50-, even 100-fold with zero work on your part. What's not to like?

Yet, while we all know the potential in stocks, I believe we all know in our heart of hearts that stocks never move in a straight line up.

Years and years of growth by the laws of nature have to be matched with years of rest and reprieve. We had 20 years of stocks going up, up, and up, and 20 years of volatility to follow. When you have a year like 2017, when the market triples its long-term rate, you have to have years like 2018, where the market has to stabilize.

That's why I've spent the last 20 years of my career teaching people that return has two components. Total return equals growth plus income. And the more you age, the less time you have to recover when growth turns into a loss.

MY MISSION

Thirteen years ago, I realized that my influence as an independent advisor could only reach so far. That's why I founded Advisors' Academy in 2006 so I could reach more people.

Advisors' Academy[75] is a network of financial advisors all over the nation who have made it their fiduciary responsibility to reposition their clients' portfolios in a way that will help them generate income during retirement, while avoiding the risks that come with secular bear markets.

It was a step in the right direction.

However, after some time, I realized I needed to do more.

For the next eight years, I saw some success with Advisors' Academy, convincing dozens of financial advisors across the country that they need to adopt an income-focused retirement strategy for their clients who were at or near retirement age. But what I quickly realized is that most financial advisors are unsure how to invest their clients' money without resorting to the same, outdated strategies, such as the stock market model. That's because they haven't understood the true nature of the market environment we've been in since the year 2000. They haven't realized we're still in a secular bear market.

That's why I founded Sound Income Strategies[76] in 2014, a program that equips our network of financial advisors with the precise strategies they need to invest their clients' money. Through Sound Income Strategies, we are able to generate income in the form of interest and dividends for our clients in retirement, allowing them to live solely off the income their investments generate without ever touching their principal, and thereby preserving their nest egg for their later years.

Now, I've gone one step further by launching our most ambitious project through the Retirement Income Store. Just as department stores popped up to meet the consumer demands of a growing population, The Retirement Income Store's purpose is to meet the investment demands of a population that needs income to last their entire lifetime with less risk.

STARING DOWN THE BARREL OF A GUN

The problem we have right now is that, as members of the Income Generation, we are at a crossroad.

As people who are at or near retirement, we've saved up enough that we're about ready to retire. We don't have enough that we can survive another 50 percent crash as we saw in 2000 and 2008, however.

If the market keeps going up and up for the next several years and we are indeed in the middle of a new secular bull market, it will be the first time in modern history we broke three world records in regard to the stock market. It would be the first time we escaped a secular bear market with less than three major drops; it would be the shortest secular bear market in history at just 13 years, nearly four years shorter than the current record set in 1982; and it would be the first time P/E ratios never once dropped into the single digits.

Chart P

I think the likelihood of us breaking all three of those records is unlikely, especially considering the drastic actions our central banks have taken to get the economy moving after the financial crisis, the financial engineering corporations have used to inflate their stock prices, and our historically high levels of debt.

If our economy were truly healthy, we wouldn't have rising deficits and we wouldn't have one of the highest debt-to-GDP ratios in history.

> *Caption: As of the third quarter of 2018, U.S. debt is equivalent to 104.15 percent of GDP. The debt-to-GDP ratio averaged 61.70 percent from 1940 until 2017, reaching an all time high of 118.90 percent in 1946 and a record low of 31.71 in 1981. It is no coincidence that the lowest levels were reached at the bottom of the last secular bear market, before a new 20-year bull market began in the 1980s and 1990s. High levels suggest we are still in the throes of a long-term secular bear market.*

I could be wrong. Anything's possible. And there are a lot of folks who think we're in the clear. Remember, human beings are optimistic by nature to a fault.

I for one am not a betting man and I have a great deal of respect for history. I also believe that patterns that have existed for centuries tend to repeat themselves. After all, math doesn't lie. If you don't believe there's some level of order to the universe, travel up north during the winter and find the nearest snowflake.

I'VE BEEN RIGHT BEFORE

Fact is, the last two times the markets crashed I called it within months of it happening. The signs were as obvious then as they are now.

I truly believe that if it weren't for the artificial forces holding the market up, we would have seen another 40 to 50 percent crash, at least, and maybe, maybe we could breathe easy knowing another secular bull market is on the rise. But we've delayed the inevitable to such an extent that, when it finally does happen, the reckoning will be dire.

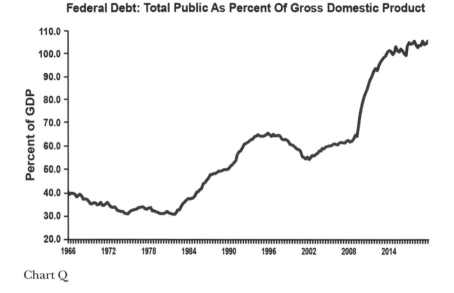

Chart Q

For years, we had artificially low rates propping the market up. When the Federal Reserve started to raise rates, central banks around the world ramped up their easing, causing money to flood into the U.S. capital market. Then, Donald Trump was elected president and pushed through an aggressive tax policy that transformed the U.S. from having the highest corporate tax rates in the world to some of the most competitive. So we got the Trump bump.

What next?

What will be the next force to drive the market higher?

Because none of these forces I just listed were fundamental.

They had nothing to do with middle-class consumers going about their lives, starting businesses, bolstering the economy, and investing their money in stocks.

Again, the biggest buyer of U.S. stocks for the last several years has been U.S. corporations themselves. Retail investors like you and me don't even factor into the equation. What's next? The Federal Reserve buying stocks too?

All of these factors lead me to believe that the next few years could be rough. I can't say for sure that it will be worse than 2008 but I'm not ruling it out, either.

That's why I'm aggressively pushing the Retirement Income Store forward.

This is a very ambitious and I believe very important project. Until recently, most investors simply didn't have the right alternatives when it comes to investing their money. That's why so many people are willing to accept the risk of investing in stocks, unaware of the vast opportunities in alternative investments and the advisors that specialize in them.

To be sure, that pool of advisors is limited, which is why I'm fighting tooth and nail against the financial establishment to build out a national infrastructure dedicated to us through the Retirement Income Store. When you boil it all down, the average financial advisor is chasing after the people with a lot of zeros at the end of their bank account. That leaves fewer and fewer advisors left over for the rest of the population, and fewer still who are comfortable wading into the pool of bonds and bond-like investments.

That's why my mission is to provide an income solution for the average investor. And rather than settle for average results, we're discarding this notion that "you get what you pay for" by providing institutional-style investing, the kind Wall Street provides to its wealthiest clients, and bringing it to everyday people. Except instead of the "Growth," we're focusing on the "Income." And instead of charging them the typical Wall Street fees, we're doing it for a price that's affordable for anyone.

WHY NOW?

The question you might have is: Why has no one else tried to do something like this? With such a large vacuum in the financial industry for folks who want a reasonable rate of return with less risk, why has no one tried to carve out their niche in the industry as I have?

The reason is that it's extremely hard to do on a large scale.

For one, there's more money in it for stock advisors than there is for bond advisors. Since there's a higher potential return when it comes to stocks, there's a higher fee. And since stock advisors get paid more in fees, there are more people who want to do it.

Secondly, stock advisors attract higher-net-worth clients. That's because they can promise the *potential* for higher returns. Since every advisor wants to catch the big fish client, there are more advisors chasing after them than there are everyday clients.

Finally, very few people understand the complex rules of investing in bonds and bond-like investments. Most of the advisors working today were brought up in the '80s and '90s bull market when stocks were the only game in town.

I've personally been dedicated to the world of bond and bond-like investments for the last 20 years. I made the switch in late 1999 when I became convinced that the financial universe had collectively lost its mind in the tech bubble. I knew stocks were expensive beyond reason and due for a massive correction. Within a year we saw the worst financial crash since the Great Depression.

So I knew I made the right choice. My clients who were hesitant at first later came to thank me for quite literally saving their finances. But I also knew enough about history to know that the financial landscape would be much different going forward.

When the market crashed in 1929 after the financial euphoria of the Roaring '20s, it wasn't until 1954 before stocks reached a new high, marking 25 years of zero growth.

A quarter century gone.

So, I suspected we could expect the same after the 2000 crash. After all, that's the nature of a secular bear market. It takes two decades at least before we're in the clear.

That's why I began telling everyone I knew that there was a better way.

I started from my office in Westbrook, Connecticut, and began doing educational workshops all over the state. I told people you don't have to devote all your assets to the growth. You can invest in the income instead. I told them that it would not only give them a steadier rate of return, but a more consistent one considering the market would likely crash again.

But I eventually had to come to terms with the fact that I could only do so much good on my own.

I realized I had to build a larger network of advisors if my message was to make any sort of significant impact.

As mentioned, it was a step in the right direction. Today, Advisors' Academy is thriving, with advisors across the country, many of whom are media names in their own right. If you read the dedication of this book, it's easy to see the network of advisors around the country who first joined me at Advisors' Academy and are as passionate about the income message as I am. Separate from our work at Advisors' Academy, we all meet together with our familes at least once a year. We are as passionate about getting this message of income out to the world today as we were way back in 2006. There is still a lot of work to do. We truly want to reach 7 out of 10 Baby Boomers with this message despite the fact that America has been brainwashed with mutual funds and the market. It's an ongoing fight.

For one, people don't like change. Bonds aren't as sexy. They're not as easy to sell. Folks don't get how they work. They're too hard to invest in. There's not as much money in it for the advisor. And it requires a certain level of personnel that most small advisory offices simply aren't equipped to take on.

At the end of the day, most advisors just want to check off a box. They want to get credit for offering their clients *some* exposure to bonds through bond mutual funds. As mentioned, these have all the problems of investing in stocks and none of the advantages of bonds.

Yes, the regulatory authorities require the advisor to give you a prospectus on that bond fund so you understand the risks. Problem is, each prospectus is about 100 pages long and is written by lawyers. And what's a lawyer's job? It's to make bad things sound good. It's to overwhelm you with enough jargon and legal disclaimers that you throw your hands up in the air and sign whatever you need to move on with your life. Somewhere in that prospectus will be a tiny little disclaimer that says you could lose all your money. But who has the time to read through a hundred pages of boring text?

Seriously, it's not even good bathroom reading.

That's why the average Joe is not going to read it. Even those who are more inclined with the ways of the law don't have the time. We've all got lives.

As a result, most clients are going to put their faith in the financial advisor who put them in a bond fund. After all, the financial advisor has a "fiduciary duty" to their clients.

The goal, if you're investing in bonds, is to protect your money. It's to get a reasonable rate of return, lower than stocks, but much better than leaving your money in a savings account, and to rest assured that your money is still there when you need it.

Yet, bond funds can't offer you that security. And your average financial advisor either doesn't know the difference or knows he isn't experienced enough to invest your money in bonds directly.

Now, he doesn't *have* to invest your money in bond funds. He can at least put your money in U.S. Treasury bonds. That way, you can get a guaranteed yield of about 3 percent. Three percent is not going to cut it.

If the financial advisor doesn't have experience in bonds, bond funds or bottom-of-the-barrel-yielding bonds are the best he is going to be able to get you.

It's fundamentally an issue of supply and demand.

There's a demand for good income investments that consistently yield in the 4- to 5-, and even 6-percentage range. And while they are out there, most at-and-near retirees don't know where to find an advisor who can give them the proper exposure to these investments, because there aren't that many advisors out there who know how to do it, or have the time to learn and dedicate their time to it.

So, they do the least possible work for the greatest possible gain, for them, putting your money in bond funds knowing full well that technically you could lose all your money. And since they gave you a prospectus that says this somewhere in a textbook-sized document littered with nonsensical financial jargon, they're off the hook. If you lose your money, there's nothing you can do about it. The advisor did everything he needed to protect himself in case you get angry and want to sue.

This is the situation the average American faces.

The situation is completely different if you're a person with $5 million in your bank account. If you have money, and a lot of it, people will work for it. And they won't just do the least amount of work for it, because there's more money in it for them.

If you have that kind of money, it's a lot easier to go out and hire a manager who will do most of what we do. They're at least going to buy you individual bonds and I'm not just talking U.S. Treasuries. They may not be able to do 100 percent of what we do, but they're at least going to do the minimum, and they're going to do a better job than the average financial advisor catering to the average person with far less money.

That's good if you have $5 million and want to put a couple million in bonds.

But what if you have $1 million and you want to put $500,000 of it in bonds?

You're not going to find that person.

Unless you're a part of a larger income-based advisory network like ours that has the right infrastructure, the right resources, and the right personnel, it's very hard to find an advisor who can make a living investing their clients' capital in bonds and bond-like investments exclusively.

That's why an investor who is at or near retirement who wants to take some risk off the table is going to be encouraged to downplay the negatives when they invest with an advisor who doesn't know a lot about bonds, and that's if they're even aware of it. Humans are fundamentally optimistic people by nature. If a legal document says we could technically lose all of our money, we assume that will never happen to us. If we invest in a stock that has x, y, and z going for it, we think we'll double our money or more. That's why most investors will minimize the fact that, somewhere in the conversation.

Worse, you have a generation of financial advisors who are stuck in the '80s and '90s mentality who really, *really* want to make their clients 10 or 15 percent. They want to beat the market. It will make them more marketable, making it easier to attract more clients with deeper pockets.

Their business model is not bonds. It's not conservative investments that will keep you safe. It's full-out and risk-on. They made their bed that they want to be the orthopedic surgeon instead of the chiropractor, and they know it's really hard to be both.

That's why I was only able to make so much impact with Advisors' Academy alone. We are a band of a few good men, but when it came down to it, our impact was limited. Only so many advisors wanted to do what we were doing. Fewer still knew how.

So, that's why I decided to up the ante. In 2014, when Janet Yellen said she would begin raising interest rates, shifting the direction of the bond market for the first time in more than 30 years, I quickly set up a second business, Sound Income Strategies, so the advisors network I'd established through Advisors' Academy could focus on spreading the message, while my internal team handled the day-to-day task of portfolio management. That way, I could attract even more advisors who were originally hesitant, because their specialization in stocks stopped being a variable that was standing in the way of making the leap.

But with Sound Income Strategies, our advisors network didn't have to worry about that. We would invest their clients' money for them, and we did it without charging a second set of fees. Even better, the one fee we did charge was less than they'd get from a typical advisor who put their money in stocks.

With this strategy, we were able to bring more and more advisors into our fold. They could focus on doing what they did best, attracting new clients, while my team at Sound Income Strategies focused on the more technical details.

But there was still one big problem.

Most advisors still didn't want to make the switch because, no matter how you slice it, there's more money in stocks than there is in bonds.

I don't have that problem. As one of the largest offices in the world dedicated to the world of bond and bond-like investments, I have a large enough infrastructure that I can focus on that world exclusively and do it well. Think of it like the difference between a Mercedes dealer and a Honda dealer. Sure, the Mercedes dealer will make more money per vehicle. But if you focus on being the *best* Honda dealer, and sell a lot of them, you get enough money coming in that you don't really care that you're not selling a luxury vehicle.

But most *salesmen* don't want to sell a Honda. They want to sell a Mercedes because there's more money in it for them. There's more commission.

So what do you do about that?

You go direct. You go to the consumer.

I've been doing this to an extent for several years now with my television show, *The Income Generation,* on Newsmax TV, where I've been fortunate enough to speak with the most important financial minds of our time such as Jim Rogers[77], Robert J. Shiller[78], Marc Faber[79], Steve Forbes Jr.[80], Peter Schiff[81], Dan Gainor[82], George Gilder[83], and many more. I bring these people on my show to talk about the issues facing the Income Generation today. I want to do more than just educate; I want to provide the solution.

The problem with Advisors' Academy is that my goal was to educate advisors on the advantage of investing for the "Income" instead of the "Growth." But most advisors aren't willing to make the switchover. Sure, we settled one of their concerns—investing for the "I" is too hard—and set up Sound Income Strategies. That way they could just focus on getting new clients. But the main problem was still there—there's more money in it for advisors who choose the "G" than there is for those who choose the "I."

I don't mean to vilify the typical financial advisor. Yours is probably a good guy. The problem is much deeper than any one person. It's systemic. It comes down to Wall Street's endless greed and thirst for more power and wealth. Your typical financial advisor is just trying to pay the mortgage, fund his children's college tuition, and put food on the table. So he goes where the money is.

But it doesn't change the fact that people who are at or near retirement age need a different approach.

That's why with the Retirement Income Store, we're circumventing the world of financial advisors and bringing our message directly to the consumer population.

For the last 20 years, I've been creating an infrastructure so the members of what I call the Income Generation can get the exposure to the types of investments that offer protection, a reasonable rate of return, and diversification outside of stocks. We're taking institutional-style investing, the kind you normally have to have millions of dollars to get access to, and bringing it to the average investor.

We literally have several analysts whose sole job it is to sit in front of a computer all day monitoring Bloomberg Terminals for swap opportunities in the bond market that require you to be able to pounce on them in a moment's notice. And rather than pile one fee on top of another in a murky pool of mutual funds, we charge one fee, and in many cases that fee is a lot less than you'll find anywhere else.

That's what we offer in a nutshell.

And as difficult as it might seem to believe, it's completely revolutionary. No one to my knowledge has done anything on this kind of scale.

I've already explained that most advisors are more comfortable sticking to stocks because:

1. It's what they're familiar with; and
2. There's more money in it for them.

There is one other hurdle. It's also very expensive.

The fact of the matter is that most financial advisors can't afford a Bloomberg Terminal like we can. And if they can, they probably can't afford to hire a CFA to sit in front of it for eight hours a day monitoring opportunities in the bond market. The Bloomberg Terminal alone costs tens of thousands a year. A good CFA will run you well into the six figures.

That's just the start of it.

We launched The Retirement Income Store with more than 20 offices immediately available to consumers throughout the country. We are growing and we want to grow even faster so that we have an office or storefront in every state.

Our big fat hairy audacious goal is to reach 7 out of 10 people over the age of 50. I've already convinced an army of advisors to join in the mission. I can only do it if investors and advisors alike are willing to experience it, and then spread the word about INCOME nationally. With 300 million people in the country, I suspect our message will spread like wildfire.

I think the timing is perfect. The national mood is changing.

People on both the right and the left are aware something is horribly wrong in our country. The disparity between the upper and lower classes has gotten out of hand. Capitalism only works when it is tempered with a healthy democracy and right now there are too few people holding the bulk of the wealth, who are calling the shots in Washington. In that sort of environment, more money flows to the top and less of it flows into the middle and lower classes.

That's why the Retirement Income Store is so important and couldn't come at a better time.

We're in a situation today where the top 10 percent of the population holds 75 percent of the wealth, and the top 20 percent holds 87 percent. That means that 80 percent of the population holds just 13 percent of the wealth. That is not the stuff that a thriving economy and democracy are made of.

I don't care what party you are, it's not good.

The people are getting sick of it.

Like him or hate him, people voted for Donald Trump because they believed he would "drain the swamp." They voted for him because he offered something different, at least in theory. He at least was calling attention to the problems whereas other politicians were going on pretending that everything was hunky dory.

And this is all while the stock market is at its highest in human history. There's a lot of money on the table, but it doesn't matter when it all flows to the people who already had plenty of money to begin with.

In order to retire, most people need a bare minimum of 50 to 70 percent of their preretirement salary. In order to comfortably retire, you need a lot more. And yet only 22.4 percent of Baby Boomers age 55 and up have $300,000 or more in savings. More than 45 percent have less than $10,000 saved.

Millennials - Gen X - Baby Boomers - Median Savings For Retirement

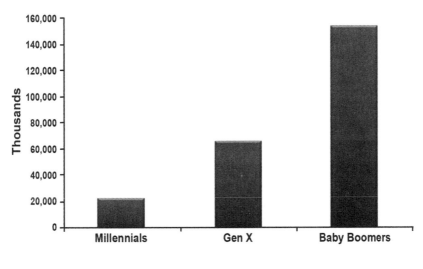

Chart R

The situation gets worse when the affluent have the resources available to them to invest their money smarter and more safely and the average person doesn't. With that advantage, the rich are going to keep getting richer and there's going to be an even bigger disparity between the classes. That's not good for anybody. Without a thriving middle class, eventually the upper class will collapse. The only reason companies like Amazon,[84] Apple,[85] and Netflix [6] have made people at the top so wealthy is because people like and buy their products.

So, yes, maybe I'm not making as much money as I would if I had stayed in the world of the "G." Fact is, there's more

money in stocks. In my mind, members of the Income Generation don't need them. Just as we don't need a bunch of Mercedes dealers selling luxury sports cars to folks who don't need
them. We need more people selling Hondas because they're
safe, less expensive to buy, and heck, they hold their value. But
I view what I'm doing as a public good. As things stand today,
there is simply no national movement dedicated to helping
members of the Income Generation, the 74 million Baby
Boomers who are at or near retirement, get the income they
actually need.

Too often I hear stories of crooked advisors who swindle
unsuspecting retirees out of their money by investing it in
risky securities they have no business being in. Trouble is, we
don't have a financially educated society, so most people aren't
aware when they're getting duped. It's criminal.

That's why I'm working to turn Wall Street's game on its
head by bringing high-level institutional income investing, the
kind you normally need $5 million to get access to, people
with a lot less in assets. Heck, we'll work with you if you only
have $100,000. No one else may want you, but we do, because
it's the right thing to do. There's strength in numbers. A society is only as strong as its weakest link, and damn it, I want to
do my part to help our middle class get back to something we
as a people can be proud of.

With the Retirement Income Store, we're trying to reedu-
cate the public in a way that financial advisors aren't going to
do because there's no incentive for them. We're trying to teach
people that there's an alternative to leaving your money sitting
in stocks just waiting for something bad to happen, because
Wall Street says "stocks always go up in the long run." That's
fine if you're 20 or 30. If you're 50 or 60, it doesn't work. That's
why we're trying to show people there *are* advisors you can
trust to be good stewards of your money. We want people to

realize that total return is about the "I" and the "G," not just the "G," and that when the growth is not available, or extremely risky as it is today, that you have to focus on the income.

IT'S TIME TO MAKE THE SWITCH

Breaking a habit is never easy. Yes, you'll always hear the stories about how grandpa or some distant uncle quit his addiction to nicotine cold turkey, but for the average person, the path to recovery is one of blood, sweat, and tears.

They say the worst impediment to overcoming addiction, and staying in remission, is being overexposed to the drug you're addicted to. That's a problem our generation is faced with every day.

We've all heard the stories about people who bought stocks that doubled or tripled. Perhaps that's happened to you on a few occasions. When that happens, it's like winning the lottery, and as we've discussed, there isn't much of a difference between hitting the slots and speculating in the market; it's gambling. When your money doubles, it feels like the jackpot.

It reminds me of the first time we got a casino in Connecticut on the Indian reservation. I went just to check the place out, and this guy comes up and starts badgering me about how he just won the big jackpot. His "big" jackpot was $750. My friends and I figured he probably spent $1,200 to get it.

It doesn't matter. Everyone likes to remember that one big win. When we get it, our addiction feeds itself. We're like a hamster on a wheel. For me, it doesn't matter how many times I shoot a 110 on the golf course. I'm always going to remember that one birdie, and the other time I sunk that 20-foot putt, and I'm going to keep playing until I do it again. Except it will never be enough.

I get how addiction works, but eventually, we all have to come to terms with our addiction. If we forget the lessons we learned from Enron[87] and WorldCom,[88] you know what they say, those who forget history are doomed to repeat it.

I believe in the next three to five years we're going to see a mass exodus of people ditching stocks as people in our generation finally come to terms with the fact that the stock market is not the vehicle that is going to protect their retirement nest egg. That's why I'm working to build out a national infrastructure for income seekers and income advisors through the Retirement Income Store that can accommodate this growing demand.

After all, we are the generation that, in many ways, defined what it means to be an American. Our generation is the one that has seen the greatest middle class in world history. We're the one that has come the closest to realizing the American Dream. Many of us have even achieved it.

We are the trendsetters, and I believe in the coming years we are going to set a new trend as more and more members of the Income Generation turn to the income for their investment returns.

I have no delusions that it will be easy. In fact, establishing the Retirement Income Store is the greatest personal undertaking of my career. I have set a personal goal to reach 7 out of every 10 members of the Income Generation.

But, I believe our generation is ready to make that switch.

And I can only do it with your help.

As you've learned, I can't force financial advisors to make the switch if they don't want to. That means the only way forward is educating the public so they demand a better service.

My hope is that you'll spread the word.

My hope is that you'll talk to your friends, family, and colleagues about this.

My hope is that you'll go to your financial advisors and ask

them, "Are you a member of the Retirement Income Store?" We
have franchised our business model so independent financial
advisors can co-market themselves under our brand. For instance,
my operation in Westbrook, Connecticut, Scranton Financial
Group, isn't just a stand-alone business. It is now "Scranton Financial Group, a Retirement Income Store."

I want this to sweep across the nation.

I want to bring institutional-style investing to the average
investor.

I want to radically disrupt the current financial system that
thinks the "G" is the end-all, be-all, to investing while they
currently toss the "I" in the kitchen sink.

I want people to have the best retirement they can possibly
have.

And I want to reach as many people as possible before the
stock market takes another nosedive and makes it impossible
for people who are at or near retirement to ever retire. I don't
want you to have to work well into your golden years. If you
worked hard for your money, I want to help you keep it. I don't
want it to be squandered because of Wall Street's greed.

But I can't do it alone.

People who are stuck in their ways are stubborn.

Advisors who have been doing things the same way for decades
aren't going to change unless a chorus of voices demand it.

We all have someone in our life who is impossibly stubborn.
Someone who doesn't listen to reason and thinks he or she is
smarter than he or she actually is. They're the most infuriat-
ing type of person. Because the smarter you think you are, the
more fixed you are in your way of thinking. The less receptive
you are to change.

That's what the average financial advisor is like.

They're exuding confidence and they need to. They need to
be able to get a person to trust their life savings with them.

For better or worse, people who exude confidence are very

persuasive. We're more likely to trust people who seem sure of themselves. In my 20 years as an income-oriented advisor, I've discovered something interesting.

The average client is a lot smarter when it comes to this stuff than the average advisor.

Now that doesn't mean I recommend you take your retirement into your hands and start investing your money on your own.

It just means that when I present the evidence to clients, they're typically more receptive. They say, "That makes sense." Investing for the income makes sense to them.

When I present it to the average advisor, however, they short-circuit. It's cognitive dissonance to them. Cognitive dissonance is when you present someone with evidence that runs contrary to their hardwired line of thinking. It's a funny thing to watch, because they usually get very defensive. They shift in their seat, cross their arms, furrow their brow. It's because they're stubborn.

That's why I'm bringing the Retirement Income Store to you.

To heck with all the lazy advisors who are so addicted to their '80s and '90s business model and unwilling to learn something that makes better financial sense.

If the average client understands this stuff makes sense and the average advisor is too stubborn to accept it, my hope and prayer is that you, the public as smart, financially informed people, might be able to knock some sense into your financial advisor. If I can't, maybe you can.

That's how we're going to reach our big hairy audacious goal of bringing our message to 7 out of 10 Income Generation members. In order to educate advisors, we need to start with the investor. Because the typical advisor doesn't care what I have to say. They don't work for me. They work for you. You pay them, and money talks.

LOOK OUT FOR A RETIREMENT INCOME STORE NEAR YOU

I've spent the last 20 years beating my head against the wall trying to educate the advisor. I wrote this book because at some point I failed to realize that, despite my best efforts, most financial advisors wanted to continue drinking Wall Street's Kool-Aid. Even if I made it easier, they don't want to do the "I"; they want to focus on the "G" for all the reasons we've gone over. Now, I'm going beyond that. After 20 years I'm finally giving up on trying to persuade the advisor that there's a better way because I think you'll be more receptive to my message. I'm confident that, after reading everything, you'll see the benefit of investing in the "I" and not the "G" a lot more than an advisor who's still suffering from stock market addiction.

Again, the reason why we call it a Retirement Income "Store" is because it should be as easy as buying coffee. It should be as easy as going on Amazon and ordering a pair of shoes. It's right there. You walk into a store, or open up a web browser, and it's sitting there waiting for you. I firmly believe that investing for income should be just as easy. Because just as consumers also need things like coffee, clothes, shoes, groceries, they also need income. And yet we have an entire financial system dedicated to some perverted sense of the American Dream, that if they just buy stocks and hold on long enough they'll come out the other side richer.

Something's got to change. We can't go through our whole lives suffering from stock market addiction or else we're going to wind up like a junky addicted to heroin on the streets, putting every last dollar in jeopardy for the next stock market hit, the next escape, the hope for a better life.

It's time we create a new financial establishment that caters to middle America and not the 1 percent. It's time we get back to the basics and invest the way our parents did before we all got caught up in the financial insanity of the '80s and '90s bull market.

That's our goal with The Retirement Income Store—to create a new standard by which clients come together to hold their financial advisors accountable. I've franchised the Retirement Income Store so that any financial office can call us up and brand themselves with our message so prospective clients know they mean business, and know that they're going to invest their money the right way.

I'm doing this now because, as a person in his 50s, I'm starting to think about the kind of legacy I want to leave behind. I think I've been a pioneer of sorts these last 20 years, embarking into uncharted waters and forging a path in the darkness hoping to bring some light to a financially insane world.

Sure, we may have lower profit margins at the Retirement Income Store than the big Wall Street firm charging two or three times as much in fees, but I don't care anymore. I want to do what I think is right. I want to do my part to help make the world a better place.

Look, I don't pretend for a moment that this book has completely persuaded you to reposition your financial life according to our model. My only hope is that you'll take what I've said to heart and at least start a conversation about it. I hope you'll share this book with others, and share it with your financial advisor and ask him what he thinks about all this.

If nothing else, I hope this book inspires you to head over to www.retirementincomestore.com to find a Retirement Income Store in your area and at least have a conversation. Go in with no expectations, have a conversation with one of our trusted advisors, and see what you think. If you like the idea of keeping the money you've worked so hard to accumulate, if you like the idea of sidestepping the next market crash, if you like the idea of stable returns in an otherwise unstable market, then I ask you to have an open mind. I ask you to share our story with others. And I ask you to do everything within your power to create the retirement for yourself that you deserve.

NOTES

1. **Google LLC:** Was founded in 1998 by Larry Page and Sergey Brin
    while they were Ph.D. students at Stanford University in Califor-
    nia. Together they own about 14 percent of its shares and control
    56 percent of the stockholder voting power through super voting
    stock. They incorporated Google as a privately held company on
    September 4, 1998. An initial public offering (IPO) took place on
    August 19, 2004, and Google moved to its headquarters in Moun-
    tain View, California, nicknamed the Googleplex. In August 2015,
    Google announced plans to reorganize its various interests as a
    conglomerate called Alphabet Inc. Google is Alphabet's leading
    subsidiary and will continue to be the umbrella company for Al-
    phabet's Internet interests. Sundar Pichai was appointed CEO of
    Google, replacing Larry Page who became the CEO of Alphabet.

    https://en.wikipedia.org/wiki/Google

2. **Dot-com Bubble:** Also known as the dot-com boom, the tech bub-
    ble, and the Internet bubble; was a historic speculative bubble and
    period of excessive speculation mainly in the United States that oc-
    curred roughly from 1995 to 2000, a period of extreme growth in
    the use and adoption of the Internet. The Nasdaq Composite stock
    market index, which included many Internet-based companies,
    peaked in value on March 10, 2000, before crashing. The burst
    of the bubble, known as the dot-com crash, lasted from March 11,
    2000, to October 9, 2002.

    https://en.wikipedia.org/wiki/Dot-com_bubble

    Financial Crisis of 2007–2008: Also known as the global financial
    crisis and the 2008 financial crisis, is considered by many
    economists to have been the most serious financial crisis since

the Great Depression of the 1930s. It began in 2007 with a crisis
in the subprime mortgage market in the United States, and
developed into a full-blown international banking crisis with the
collapse of the investment bank Lehman Brothers on September
15, 2008. Excessive risk-taking by banks such as Lehman Brothers
helped to magnify the financial impact globally. Massive bail-outs
of financial institutions and other palliative monetary and fiscal
policies were employed to prevent a possible collapse of the world
financial system.

https://en.wikipedia.org/wiki/Financial_crisis

3. **The Income Generation:** Sound Income Strategies was found-
    ed by David Scranton (CLU, ChFC, CFP®, CFA, MSFS). Dave
    has gained much notoriety during his 30 years in the industry as
    an advisor who is particularly protective of his clients' assets. For
    the past 20 years, he has specialized in the universe of income-
    generating savings and investment strategies. Sound Income Strat-
    egies is a Registered Investment Advisory firm specializing in the
    active management of income-generating portfolios. With our
    years of industry experience, we focus on maximizing the value of
    your income portfolio and help you build a retirement plan that
    delivers dependable income, growth potential, and, most impor-
    tantly, defense against damaging losses. As a Registered Investment
    Advisory firm, we honor our fiduciary responsibility. As spelled out
    in the U.S. Investment Advisers Act of 1940, our goal is to always act
    and serve in the best interest of our clients.

    http://theincomegeneration.com/

4. **Federal Reserve:** The Federal Reserve System is the central bank
    of the United States. It performs five general functions to promote
    the effective operation of the U.S. economy and, more generally,
    the public interest. The Federal Reserve:

    - Conducts the nation's monetary policy to promote
      maximum employment, stable prices, and moderate
      long-term interest rates in the U.S. economy.
    - Promotes the stability of the financial system and seeks
      to minimize and contain systemic risks through active
      monitoring and engagement in the U.S. and abroad.
    - Promotes the safety and soundness of individual fi-
      nancial institutions and monitors their impact on the
      financial system as a whole.

    https://www.federalreserve.gov/aboutthefed/files/pf_1.pdf

5. *Life* **Magazine:** Was an American magazine published weekly until 1972, as an intermittent "special" until 1978, and as a monthly from 1978 to 2000. During its golden age from 1936 to 1972, *Life* was a wide-ranging weekly general interest magazine known for the quality of its photography.

   https://en.wikipedia.org/wiki/Life_(magazine)

6. **Industrial Revolution:** In modern history, the process of change from an agrarian and handicraft economy to one dominated by industry and machine manufacturing. This process began in Britain in the 18th century and from there spread to other parts of the world. Although used earlier by French writers, the term *Industrial Revolution* was first popularized by the English economic historian Arnold Toynbee (1852–83) to describe Britain's economic development from 1760 to 1840. Since Toynbee's time the term has been more broadly applied.

   https://www.britannica.com/event/Industrial-Revolution

7. **Macy's:** No one would have guessed that the small, fancy dry goods store that opened on the corner of 14th Street and 6th Avenue in New York City in 1858 would grow to be one of the largest retailers in the world. But after several failed retail ventures, Rowland Hussey Macy's determination and ingenuity paid off at the age of 36 with the launch of R.H. Macy & Co. He adopted a red star as his symbol of success, dating back to his days as a sailor. First-day sales totaled $11.06 but by the end of the first full year, sales grossed approximately $85,000. By 1877, R.H. Macy & Co. had become a full-fledged department store occupying the ground space of 11 adjacent buildings.

   https://www.macysinc.com/about-us/macysinc-history/overview/default.aspx

8. **Marshall Field & Company:** Traces its antecedents to a dry goods store opened at 137 Lake Street in Chicago, Illinois, in 1852 by Potter Palmer (1826–1902), eponymously named P. Palmer & Company. In 1856, 21-year-old Marshall Field (1834–1906) moved to the booming midwestern city of Chicago on the southwest shores of Lake Michigan from Pittsfield, Massachusetts, and found work at the city's then-largest dry goods firm—Cooley, Wadsworth & Company.

   https://en.wikipedia.org/wiki/Marshall_Fieldpercent27s

9. **The Retirement Income Store:** Sound Income Strategies is a Registered Investment Advisory firm specializing in the active management of income-generating portfolios. With our years of industry experience, we focus on maximizing the value of your income portfolio and help you build a retirement plan that delivers dependable income, growth potential, and, most importantly, defense against damaging losses. As a Registered Investment Advisory firm, we honor our fiduciary responsibility. As spelled out in the U.S. Investment Advisers Act of 1940, our goal is to always act and serve in the best interest of our clients.

   https://soundincomestrategies.com/retirement-income-store/

10. **Albert Einstein (March 14, 1879, to April 18, 1955):** Was a German mathematician and physicist who developed the special and general theories of relativity.

   https://www.biography.com/people/albert-einstein-9285408

11. **Bristol, Connecticut:** Is a suburban city located in Hartford County, Connecticut, United States, 20 miles (32 km) southwest of Hartford. The city is also 120 miles southwest from Boston, and approximately 100 miles northeast of New York City. As of the 2010 census, the population of the city was 60,477.

   https://en.wikipedia.org/wiki/Bristol,_Connecticut

12. **Otto Von Leopold, Prince of Bismarck:** *Old Age and Disability Insurance Law of 1889*: The old age pension program, insurance equally financed by employers and workers, was designed to provide a pension annuity for workers who reached the age of 70. Unlike the accident and sickness insurance programs, this program covered all categories of workers (industrial, agrarian, artisans and servants) from the start. Also, unlike the other two programs, the principle that the national government should contribute a portion of the underwriting cost, with the other two portions prorated accordingly, was accepted without question. The disability insurance program was intended to be used by those permanently disabled. This time, the state or province supervised the programs directly.

   https://en.wikipedia.org/wiki/Otto_von_Bismarck

13. **Ida May Fuller:** Miss Fuller filed her retirement claim on November 4, 1939, having worked under Social Security for a little short of three years. While running an errand she dropped by the Rutland Social Security office to ask about possible benefits. She would

later observe: "It wasn't that I expected anything, mind you, but I knew I'd been paying for something called Social Security and I wanted to ask the people in Rutland about it." Her claim was taken by Claims Clerk, Elizabeth Corcoran Burke, and transmitted to the Claims Division in Washington, D.C. for adjudication. The case was adjudicated and reviewed and sent to the Treasury Department for payment in January 1940.

https://en.wikipedia.org/wiki/Ida_May_Fuller

14. **U.S. Bureau of Labor Statistics:** Data dated 2018, Stated that the average hours per day spent watching TV for ages 15 years and over was 2.77 hours. The average retiree ages 65 and over watched 4.37 hours per day. Those 55 to 64 years on average tuned in for about 3.23 hours.

https://www.bls.gov/charts/american-time-use/activity-leisure.htm

15. **Lump-Sum Purchase:** A lump-sum purchase occurs when several assets are acquired for a single price. Each of the assets must be recorded separately as a fixed asset in the accounting records; to do so, the purchase price is allocated among the various acquired assets based on their fair market values. This situation most commonly arises when property is purchased and the purchase price includes both land and structures.

https://www.accountingtools.com/articles/2017/5/13/lump-sum-purchase

16. **Current U.S. Inflation Rates:** The current inflation rate for the United States is 1.5 percent for the 12 months ended February 2019, as published on March 12, 2019 by the U.S. Labor Department. The next inflation update is scheduled for release on April 10, 2019 at 8:30 a.m. ET. It will offer the rate of inflation over the 12 months ended March 2019.

https://www.usinflationcalculator.com/inflation/current-inflation-rates/

17. **Federal Reserve Bank of St. Louis:** Healthy Inflation? Inflation in the healthcare industry vs. general CPI. Some components of the consumer price index have consistently, over several decades, risen faster than the rest.

https://fredblog.stlouisfed.org/2017/07/healthy-inflation/

18. **Medicare Part B:** You pay a premium each month for Part B. Your Part B premium will be automatically deducted from your benefit payment if you get benefits from one of these:

   - Social Security
   - Railroad Retirement Board
   - Office of Personnel Management

   If you don't get these benefit payments, you'll get a bill.

   Most people will pay the standard premium amount. If you're modified adjusted gross income is above a certain amount, you may pay an Income Related Monthly Adjustment Amount (IR-MAA). Medicare uses the modified adjusted gross income reported on your IRS tax return from 2 years ago. This is the most recent tax return information provided to Social Security by the IRS.

   https://www.medicare.gov/your-medicare-costs/part-b-costs

19. **The 4 Percent Rule:** Is often confused with the Multiply by 25 Rule, for obvious reasons—the 4 Percent Rule, as its name implies, also assumes a 4 percent return. The 4 Percent Rule, however, guides how much you should withdraw annually once you're retired. As the name implies, this rule of thumb says you should withdraw 4 percent of your retirement portfolio the first year.

   https://www.thebalance.com/dont-confuse-these-two-retirement-rules-of-thumb-453920

20. **IRA Traditional And Roth IRAs:** For 2019, your total contributions to all of your traditional and Roth IRAs cannot be more than:

   - $6,000 ($7,000 if you're age 50 or older), or
   - Your taxable compensation for the year, if your compensation was less than this dollar limit.

   For 2015, 2016, 2017 and 2018, you're total contributions to all of your traditional and Roth IRAs cannot be more than:

   - $5,500 ($6,500 if you're age 50 or older), or
   - Your taxable compensation for the year, if your compensation was less than this dollar limit.

   https://www.irs.gov/retirement-plans/plan-participant-employee/retirement-topics-ira-contribution-limits

21. **Monte Carlo Methods:** Are a broad class of computational algorithms that rely on repeated random sampling to obtain numerical results. Their essential idea is using randomness to solve problems that might be deterministic in principle. They are often used in

physical and mathematical problems and are most useful when it is difficult or impossible to use other approaches. Monte Carlo methods are mainly used in three problem classes: optimization, numerical integration, and generating draws from a probability distribution.

https://en.wikipedia.org/wiki/Monte_Carlo_method

22. **Russian Roulette:** Is a lethal game of chance in which a player places a single round in a revolver, spins the cylinder, places the muzzle against their head, and pulls the trigger. *Russian* refers to the supposed country of origin, and *roulette* to the element of risk-taking and the spinning of the revolver's cylinder, which is reminiscent of a spinning roulette wheel.

https://en.wikipedia.org/wiki/Russian_roulette

23. **Dollar Cost Averaging:** Dollar-cost averaging is the strategy of spreading out your stock or fund purchases, buying at regular intervals and in roughly equal amounts. So instead of buying stock in a single large purchase, you invest that same amount over a year or two years or even indefinitely, by regularly adding money to the market.

When done properly, dollar-cost averaging can have significant benefits for your portfolio. This is because the strategy "smooths" your purchase price over time and helps ensure that you're not dumping all your money in at a high point for prices.

Dollar-cost averaging can be especially powerful in a bear market, allowing you to "buy the dips," or purchase stock at low points when most investors are too afraid to buy. Committing to this strategy means that you will be investing when the market or a stock is down, and that's when investors score the best deals.

https://www.nerdwallet.com/blog/investing/dollar-cost-averaging-2/

24. **Reverse Dollar Cost Averaging:** In traditional retirement planning, you implicitly presume that stocks will earn the assumed return steadily, year in and year out. But in reality, the stock market goes through periods of sideways movements or bear markets when prices get depressed and returns are much lower than the long-term average, and then through periods of bull markets with exuberant prices and much higher than average returns. So if you wind up unlucky and run into a bear market during the early years of your retirement and continue selling the same dollar amount

of stocks, you will have to sell a lot more stocks during those years because of the lower prices than your plan anticipated. Even if the stock market recovers in the later years and provides much higher returns, you may never fully recover from the earlier damage because you will then have much less money invested in stocks on which you will earn those higher returns.

https://www.mdmag.com/journals/pmd/2004/35/1470

25. **Patrick Peason:** Has been in the financial services industry for 31 years and specializes in the unique challenges facing today's retirees and pre-retirees. In today's tough market economy, seniors need to fully understand all the various options that are currently available to assist them in protecting and growing their investment portfolios.

https://patrickpeason.fixedincomecounsel.com/about-us/our-people/

26. **The American Institute of CPAs:** As the national, professional organization for all Certified Public Accountants, the AICPA's mission is to power the success of global business, CPAs, CGMAs and specialty credentials by providing the most relevant knowledge, resources and advocacy, and protecting the evolving public interest. From financial literacy to public policy issues and peer review transparency to audit committee effectiveness, the AICPA is working to ensure that the public remains confident in the integrity, objectivity, competence and professionalism of CPAs.

https://www.aicpa.org/forthepublic.html

27. **Standard & Poor's 500 Index Fund:** Picking a fund that tracks the S&P 500 Index may seem like a simple task. After all, an index fund is designed to mirror an index's holdings, so issues such as a manager's quality or investment style don't come into play.

But it's actually harder than you might expect. There are more than 50 S&P 500 Index funds to choose from.

https://www.consumerreports.org/personal-investing/how-to-choose-an-index-fund/

28. **FanDuel:** Is a daily fantasy sports provider from the United States and bookmaker based in New York City. Originally founded in 2009, the service is the second largest DFS service in the country (behind DraftKings) based on entry fees and user base.

https://en.wikipedia.org/wiki/FanDuel

29. **Warren Buffett:** Born August 30, 1930, is an American business magnate, investor, speaker and philanthropist who serve as the chairman and CEO of Berkshire Hathaway. He is considered one of the most successful investors in the world and has a net worth of US $84.4 billion as of November 1, 2018, making him the third-wealthiest person in the world.

   https://en.wikipedia.org/wiki/Warren_Buffett

30. **Robert Kenneth Kraft:** Born June 5, 1941, is an American business-man. He is the chairman and chief executive officer of the Kraft Group, a diversified holding company with assets in paper and packaging, sports and entertainment, real estate development and a private equity portfolio. He is the owner of the National Football League's New England Patriots, Major League Soccer's New England Revolution, and Gillette Stadium, where both teams play. He also owns the Boston Uprising, the first eSports team in New England.

   https://en.wikipedia.org/wiki/Robert_Kraft

31. **Long-Term Average Market Return:** The stock market has histor-ically returned an average of 10% annually. Over nearly the last century, the stock market's average return is about 10% annually. That's what long-term investors in the stock market can expect to earn if they use the stock market model for their investments over time.

   https://www.nerdwallet.com/blog/investing/average-stock-market-return/

32. **Long-Term Growth Rate LTG:** Is an investing strategy and concept in which a security appreciates in value for a relatively long period of time, whether or not this growth begins immediately or develops gradually. Long-term growth is a relative term as investors' time horizons differ, based on their individual styles.

   https://www.investopedia.com/terms/l/longtermgrowth.asp

33. **Tech Bubble:** The bubble popping in 2000 (it was not 2001) was a lot like an avalanche. It wasn't clear exactly which snowflake was the one that put it over the tipping point, but once confidence was lost, it went very quickly.

   https://www.quora.com/What-was-the-trigger-for-the-tech-bubble-to-burst-in-2000

34. **A Secular Bear Market:** Is categorized by below average stock mar-

ket returns over a period of nearly a generation, while a cyclical bull market's average length approximates that of a business cycle. Since hitting bottom in March 2009, equities have enjoyed a nearly four-year cyclical bull market. The only question on every investor's mind should now be: is this the beginning of a new secular trend? Or, simply a cyclical divergence within a secular bear market?

https://seekingalpha.com/article/1097631-on-secular-vs-cyclical-bull-and-bear-markets

35. **Bear-Market Cycle:** Just like a secular bull market, a secular bear market is one that lasts between five and 25 years. And while the average length of a secular bear market is about 17 years, there may be smaller bull or bear markets within it. Still, the average bear market is much shorter—usually under a year—and so definitions of what constitutes a secular bear market vary.

https://www.thestreet.com/markets/what-is-a-bear-market-14713949

36. **Great Depression:** Was a severe worldwide economic depression that took place mostly during the 1930s, beginning in the United States. The timing of the Great Depression varied across nations; in most countries it started in 1929 and lasted until the late 1930s. It was the longest, deepest, and most widespread depression of the 20th century. In the 21st century, the Great Depression is commonly used as an example of how intensely the world's economy can decline.

https://en.wikipedia.org/wiki/Great_Depression

37. **Three Major Drop In Secular Bear Market:** October 9, 2002, In 2001, stock prices took a sharp downturn (some say "stock market crash" or "the Internet bubble bursting") in stock markets across the United States, Canada, Asia, and Europe.

https://en.wikipedia.org/wiki/Stock_market_downturn_of_2002

October 11, 2007, from their peaks in October 2007 until their closing lows in early March 2009, the Dow Jones Industrial Average, Nasdaq Composite and S&P 500 all suffered declines of over 50%, marking the worst stock market crash since the Great Depression era.

https://en.wikipedia.org/wiki/List_of_stock_market_crashes_and_bear_markets

38. **Dow Jones Indices LLC:** Is a joint venture between S&P Global, the CME Group, and News Corp that was announced in 2011 and later launched in 2012. It produces, maintains, licenses, and markets stock market indices as benchmarks and as the basis of investable products, such as exchange-traded funds (ETFs), mutual funds, and structured products.

https://en.wikipedia.org/wiki/Spercent26P_Dow_Jones_Indices

39. **P/E Ratios and the Tech Bubble:** *The Use of Metrics That Ignored Cash Flow.* Many analysts focused on aspects of individual businesses that had nothing to do with how they generated revenue or their cash flow.

Significantly Overvalued Stocks. In addition to focusing on unnecessary metrics, analysts used very high multipliers in their models and formulas for valuing Internet companies, which resulted in unrealistic and overly optimistic values.

https://www.moneycrashers.com/dot-com-bubble-burst/

40. **A Short-Secular Bear Market:** In January of 1966 the Dow Jones Industrial Average hit a level of 990. It would continue trading in a range of roughly 600 to 1,000 over the following 17 years. It once again reached 990 in December of 1982 before finally breaking out and heading higher. The Dow never dropped below 1,000 again. This long, drawn out sideways market is one of the ultimate devil's advocate positions for those that like to argue against stocks being a solid long-term investment. Although this was technically a sideways market we need to put some context around this time frame.

https://awealthofcommonsense.com/2014/06/1966-1982-stock-market-really-bad/

41. **Secular Bear Market History:** In secular bull markets, stocks tend to rise more than they fall with any setbacks being more than compensated for by the subsequent increase in stock prices. The most recent and famous secular bull market consists of the period between 1983 and 2000 when the United States entered into the greatest economic expansion in human history after Federal Reserve Chairman Paul Volker took a metaphorical 2x4 to the back of inflation, allowing the country to escape from the inflation-induced malaise of the 1970's.

https://www.thebalance.com/secular-bull-bear-markets-357914

42. **Single Digit P/E s and Bear Markets:** Mr. Shilling said, "Stocks will revisit single-digit P/E if there is a full-blown recession."

    https://books.google.com/
    books?id=yf4DAAAAMBAJ&pg=PA43&lpg=
    PA43&dq=single+digit+P/
    Es+and+bear+markets&source=bl&ots=iLt_PksEt-
    &sig=ACfU3U1QQBWCRPky7YtbWW4XwAX-M-VuoA&hl=en&sa=
    X&ved=2ahUKEwj_h-PkoMvhAhXJx1kKHQy_
    AOAQ6AEwEXoECAk
    QAQ#v=onepage&q=single%20digit%20P%2FEs%20and%20
    bear%20markets&f=falses

43. **Gross Domestic Product:** Is a monetary measure of the market value of all the final goods and services produced in a period of time, often annually or quarterly. Nominal GDP estimates are commonly used to determine the economic performance of a whole country or region, and to make international comparisons.

    https://en.wikipedia.org/wiki/Gross_domestic_product

44. **Guinness Book Of World Records:** Known from its inception from 1955 until 2000 as *The Guinness Book of Records* and in previous United States editions as *The Guinness Book of World Records,* is a reference book published annually, listing world records both of human achievements and the extremes of the natural world. The brainchild of Sir Hugh Beaver, the book was co-founded by brothers Norris and Ross McWhirter in Fleet Street, London in August 1954.

    https://en.wikipedia.org/wiki/Guinness_World_Records

45. **P/E Ratios:** The **price/earnings ratio** (often shortened to the **P/E ratio** or the **PER**) is the ratio of a company's share (stock) price to the company's earnings per share. The ratio is used for valuing companies and to find out whether they are overvalued or undervalued.

    https://en.wikipedia.org/wiki/Price%E2%80%93earnings_ratio

46. **Ben Shalom Bernanke:** Born December 13, 1953, is an American economist at the Brookings Institution who served two terms as Chair of the Federal Reserve, the central bank of the United States, from 2006 to 2014. During his tenure as chair, Bernanke oversaw the Federal Reserve's response to the late-2000s financial crisis. Before becoming Federal Reserve chair, Bernanke was a tenured

professor at Princeton University and chaired the department of economics there from 1996 to September 2002, when he went on public service leave.

https://en.wikipedia.org/wiki/Ben_Bernanke

47. **Quantitative Easing:** Also known as large-scale asset purchases, is an expansionary monetary policy whereby a central bank buys predetermined amounts of government bonds or other financial assets in order to stimulate the economy and increase liquidity. An unconventional form of monetary policy, it is usually used when inflation is very low or negative, and standard expansionary monetary policy has become ineffective.

https://en.wikipedia.org/wiki/Quantitative_easing

48. **Central Banks: Reserve bank** or **monetary authority** is the institution that manages the currency, money supply, and interest rates of a state or formal monetary union, and oversees their commercial banking system. In contrast to a commercial bank, a central bank possesses a monopoly on increasing the monetary base in the state, and also generally controls the printing/coining of the national currency, which serves as the state's legal tender. A central bank also acts as a lender of last resort to the banking sector during times of financial crisis. Most central banks also have supervisory and regulatory powers to ensure the solvency of member institutions, to prevent bank runs, and to discourage reckless or fraudulent behavior by member banks.

https://en.wikipedia.org/wiki/Central_bank

49. **Operation Twist:** The Federal Open Market Committee action known as Operation Twist (named for the twist dance craze of the time) began in 1961. The intent was to flatten the yield curve in order to promote capital inflows and strengthen the dollar. The Fed utilized open market operations to shorten the maturity of public debt in the open market. It performs the 'twist' by selling some of the short term debt (with three years or less to maturity) it purchased as part of the quantitative easing policy back into the market and using the money received from this to buy longer term government debt. Although this action was marginally successful in reducing the spread between long-term maturities and short-term maturities, Vincent Reinhart and others have suggested it did not continue for a sufficient period of time to be effective.

https://en.wikipedia.org/wiki/History_of_Federal_Open_

Market_Committee_actions#Operation_Twist_(1961)

50. **Nasdaq:** Is an American stock exchange. It is the second-largest stock exchange in the world by market capitalization, behind only the New York Stock Exchange located in the same city. The exchange platform is owned by NASDAQ, Inc., which also owns the Nasdaq Nordic (formerly known as OMX) and Nasdaq Baltic stock market network and several U.S. stock and options exchanges.

https://en.wikipedia.org/wiki/NASDAQ

51. **Apple Inc.:** Apple Computers, Inc. was founded on April 1, 1976, by college dropouts Steve Jobs and Steve Wozniak, who brought to the new company a vision of changing the way people viewed computers. Jobs and Wozniak wanted to make computers small enough for people to have them in their homes or offices. Simply put, they wanted a computer that was user-friendly.

https://www.loc.gov/rr/business/businesshistory/April/apple.html

52. **Longest Cyclical Bull Markets In History:** According to a general consensus, the longest bull market since World War II spanned 3,453 days on August 22, 2018. The bull market started on March 9, 2009. The three major indexes comprising the Dow Jones Industrial Average (DOW, S&P 500, and Nasdaq [NDAQ]) all increased from lows on March 9, 2009, of 6,547 points, 676 points, and 1,268 points, respectively. As of August 22, 2018, all three indexes were up to 25,822 points, 2,862 points, and 7,859 points, respectively.

https://www.thestreet.com/investing/longest-bull-market-14804308

53. **Paradigm:** Is a widely accepted example, belief or concept. An example of paradigm is evolution. An example of paradigm is the earth being round.

https://en.wikipedia.org/wiki/Paradigm

54. **Year 2000 Problem:** Also known as the Y2K problem, the Millennium bug, the Y2K bug, or Y2K, is a class of computer bugs related to the formatting and storage of calendar data for dates beginning in the year 2000. Problems were anticipated, and arose, because many programs represented four-digit years with only the final two digits—making the year 2000 indistinguishable from 1900. The assumption of a twentieth-century date in such programs could

cause various errors, such as the incorrect display of dates and the inaccurate ordering of automated dated records or real-time events.

https://en.wikipedia.org/wiki/Year_2000_problem

55. **Full Secular Bull-Bear Cycle:** Secular bull market is characterized by above average stock market returns by the S&P 500 for a long time, typically 10 to 20 years. Periodic bear markets spring up within a secular bull market until the next cyclical bull market takes over and carries the market to even higher highs. A cyclical bull market refers to one that lasts a few months to a few years.

- Consistent rise in stock prices.
- Healthy economy.
- Geographic and political certainty.

http://www.wyattresearch.com/markets/bull-markets/

Bear Market: A bear market is when the price of an investment falls over time. It begins after prices have fallen 20 percent or more from their 52-week high. For example, the Dow Jones Industrial Average hit its record high of 26,828.39 set on October 3, 2018. If it fell 20 percent to 21,462.71, it would be in a bear market.

https://www.thebalance.com/what-is-a-bear-market-difference-from-a-bull-3305814

56. **S&P 500 Average Annual Return Since 2000:** Has only risen 82%, which works out to only 3.4% per year, annualized. In the previous 18 years (1982-99), the S&P had grown 12-fold, which works out to a stunning 14.8% per year.

https://seekingalpha.com/article/4137982-s-and-p-500-gained-3_4-percent-per-year-since-2000

57. **People by Nature Are Universally Optimistic:** Despite calamities from economic recessions, wars and famine to a flu epidemic afflicting the Earth, a new study from the University of Kansas and Gallup indicates that humans are by nature optimistic. The study, to be presented May 24, 2009, at the annual meeting of the Association for Psychological Science in San Francisco, found optimism to be universal and borderless.

https://www.sciencedaily.com/releases/2009/05/090524122539.htm

58. **Federal Deposit Insurance Corporation (FDIC):** Is a United States

government corporation providing deposit insurance to depositors
in U.S. commercial banks and savings institutions. The FDIC was
created by the 1933 Banking Act, enacted during the Great Depression to restore trust in the American banking system. More than
one-third of banks failed in the years before the FDIC's creation,
and bank runs were common. The insurance limit was initially US
$2,500 per ownership category, and this was increased several times
over the years. Since the passage of the Dodd–Frank Wall Street Re-
form and Consumer Protection Act in 2011, the FDIC insures deposits in member banks up to US $250,000 per ownership category.

https://en.wikipedia.org/wiki/Federal_Deposit_Insurance_
Corporation

59. **Acquired Immunodeficiency Syndrome Epidemic:** The U.S. Center for Disease Control (CDC) publishes an article in its *Morbidity
and Mortality Weekly Report* (*MMWR*): *Pneumocystis* Pneumonia—Los
Angeles.

https://www.hiv.gov/hiv-basics/overview/history/hiv-and-aids-
timeline

60. **Tobacco-Related Mortality:** Overall mortality among both male
and female smokers in the United States is about three times
higher than that among similar people who never smoked.

https://www.cdc.gov/tobacco/data_statistics/fact_sheets/health_
effects/tobacco_related_mortality/index.htm

61. **Laws of Agency:** Is an area of commercial law dealing with a set
of contractual, quasi-contractual and non-contractual fiduciary
relationships that involve a person, called the agent, that is au-
thorized to act on behalf of another (called the principal) to
create legal relations with a third party. Succinctly, it may be
referred to as the equal relationship between a principal and an
agent whereby the principal, expressly or implicitly, authorizes
the agent to work under his or her control and on his or her
behalf. The agent is, thus, required to negotiate on behalf of the
principal or bring him or her and third parties into contractual
relationship. This branch of law separates and regulates the relationships between:
  ▪ Agents and principals (internal relationship), known
    as the principal-agent relationship;
  ▪ Agents and the third parties with whom they deal on
    their principals' behalf (external relationship); and

■ Principals and the third parties when the agents deal.

https://en.wikipedia.org/wiki/Law_of_agency

62. **General Motors Company:** Commonly referred to as General Motors (GM), is an American multinational corporation head-quartered in Detroit that designs, manufactures, markets, and distributes vehicles and vehicle parts, and sells financial services, with global headquarters in Detroit's Renaissance Center. It was originally founded by William C. Durant on September 16, 1908 as a holding company. The company is the largest American auto-mobile manufacturer, and one of the world's largest. As of 2018, General Motors is ranked #10 on the Fortune 500 rankings of the largest United States corporations by total revenue.

https://en.wikipedia.org/wiki/General_Motors

63. **Modern Portfolio Theory:** Modern Portfolio Theory, also known as MPT, can help investors choose a set of investments that comprise one portfolio. Together the investment securities combine in such a way as to reduce market risk through diversification while achieving optimal returns. Even if you find that you don't agree with the idea of modern portfolio theory, learning the basics of MPT can help you become a better investor.

https://www.thebalance.com/what-is-mpt-2466539

64. **Efficient Frontier:** A combination of assets, i.e. a portfolio, is re-ferred to as "efficient" if it has the best possible expected level of return for its level of risk (which is represented by the standard de-viation of the portfolio's return). Here, every possible combination of risky assets can be plotted in risk–expected return space, and the collection of all such possible portfolios defines a region in this space. In the absence of the opportunity to hold a risk-free asset, this region is the opportunity set (the feasible set). The positively sloped (upward-sloped) top boundary of this region is a portion of a hyperbola and is called the "efficient frontier."

https://en.wikipedia.org/wiki/Efficient_frontier

65. **Greg Melia, "The Disease of Ease" Melia Advisory Group:** Under-stands the value of every dollar and how hard people have worked to earn it. Many investors simply suggest "staying the course" at any cost, which has left many hard-working Americans with little to nothing left for retirement. With a thorough understanding of the market cycle, Melia Advisory Group is prepared to properly equip

individuals with investments that **PROVIDE INCOME, PROTECT ASSETS,** and give **PEACE OF MIND.**

http://www.meliaadvisorygroup.com/

66. **New York Stock Exchange:** (NYSE, nicknamed "The Big Board") is an American stock exchange located at 11 Wall Street, Lower Manhattan, New York City, New York. It is by far the world's largest stock exchange by market capitalization of its listed companies at US $30.1 trillion as of February 2018. The average daily trading value was approximately US $169 billion in 2013. The NYSE trading floor is located at 11 Wall Street and is composed of 21 rooms used for the facilitation of trading. A fifth trading room, located at 30 Broad Street, was closed in February 2007. The main building and the 11 Wall Street building were designated National Historic Landmarks in 1978.

https://en.wikipedia.org/wiki/New_York_Stock_Exchange

67. **Recency Effect:** Two traditional classes of theories explain the recency effect, The Dual-Store Model and Single-Store Model.

https://en.wikipedia.org/wiki/Serial-position_effect#Recency_effect

68. **Mutual Fund:** A mutual fund is a company that pools money from many investors and invests the money in securities such as stocks, bonds, and short-term debt. The combined holdings of the mutual fund are known as its portfolio. Investors buy shares in mutual funds. Each share represents an investor's part ownership in the fund and the income it generates.

https://www.investor.gov/investing-basics/investment-products/mutual-funds

69. **Bond Mutual Fund:** Mutual funds have become a preferred way to invest for millions of Americans. A mutual fund is simply a pool of money invested for you by an investment firm in a variety of instruments like stocks, bonds or government securities. Each mutual fund is different in its make-up and philosophy. A bond mutual fund is a mutual fund that invests in bonds. Bond mutual funds can contain all of one type of bond (municipal bonds, for instance) or a combination of bond types. Each bond fund is managed to achieve a stated investment objective.

http://www.finra.org/investors/bond-funds

70. **Securities and Exchange Commission:** The U.S. Securities and Exchange Commission (SEC) is an independent agency of the United States federal government. The SEC holds primary responsibility for enforcing the federal securities laws, proposing securities rules, and regulating the securities industry, the nation's stock and options exchanges, and other activities and organizations, including the electronic securities markets in the United States.

    https://en.wikipedia.org/wiki/U.S._Securities_and_Exchange_Commission

71. **The Bloomberg Terminal:** Is a computer software system provided by the financial data vendor Bloomberg L.P. that enables professionals in the financial service sector and other industries to access the *Bloomberg Professional* service through which users can monitor and analyze real-time financial market data and place trades on the electronic trading platform. The system also provides news, price quotes, and messaging across its proprietary secure network. It is well-known among the financial community for its black interface, which is not optimized for user experience but has become a recognizable trait of the service.

    https://en.wikipedia.org/wiki/Bloomberg_Terminal

72. **Large-Cap Stocks:** A company with a capitalization of more than $10 billion.

    Market capitalization (market cap) is the market value of a publicly traded company's outstanding shares. Market capitalization is equal to the share price multiplied by the number of shares outstanding. As outstanding stock is bought and sold in public markets, capitalization could be used as an indicator of public opinion of a company's net worth and is a determining factor in some forms of stock valuation.

    https://en.wikipedia.org/wiki/Market_capitalization

73. **Gallup Business Journal:** of all the important and interesting findings Dr. Kahneman and Dr. Deaton's research has uncovered, the most reported finding is that people with an annual household income of $75,000 are about as happy as anyone gets. More specifically, those with annual household incomes below $75,000 give lower responses to both life evaluation and emotional well-being questions. But people with an annual household income of more than $75,000 don't have commensurately higher levels of

emotional well-being, even though their life evaluation rating continues to increase.

https://news.gallup.com/businessjournal/150671/happiness-is-love-and-75k.aspx

74. **Global GDP, Gross World Product:** The gross world product (GWP) is the combined gross national product of all the countries in the world. Because imports and exports balance exactly when considering the whole world, this also equals the total global gross domestic product (GDP). According to the World Bank, the 2013 nominal GWP was approximately US $75.59 trillion. In 2014, according to the CIA's *World Fact-book*, the GWP was around US $78.28 trillion in nominal terms and totaled approximately 107.5 trillion international dollars in terms of purchasing power parity (PPP). The per capita PPP GWP in 2017 was approximately $17,300 according to the *World Fact-book*.

https://en.wikipedia.org/wiki/Gross_world_product

75. **Advisors' Academy:** Advisors' Academy was founded in 2007 by David J. Scranton with a vision to recruit other highly successful, motivated advisors and teach them how to achieve even higher levels of success—while always putting the interests of their clients first.

https://advisorsacademy.com/#about

76. **Sound Income Strategies:** A popular investment misconception is that "Growth" and "Return" mean the same thing. But the reality is that growth is just one component of return, income is the other. Many on Wall Street use these terms synonymously, and advisors with stock market-based business models will tell you that investing for growth is the only way to get a reasonable return on your investments. Many people also think that you can create income, or cash flow, out of growth. They believe that if their investments grow enough, they can take income from those investments and that is simply not true.

https://soundincomestrategies.com/why-us/#our-investment-approach

77. **Jim Beeland Rogers Jr.:** Born October 19, 1942, is an American businessman and financial commentator based in Singapore. Rogers is the Chairman of Rogers Holdings and Beeland Interests, Inc. Between January 1, 1999, and January 5, 2002, Rogers did another Guinness World Record journey through 116 countries, covering

245,000 kilometers with his wife, Paige Parker, in a custom-made Mercedes. The trip began in Iceland, which was about to celebrate the 1000th anniversary of Leif Eriksson's first trip to America. On January 5, 2002, they were back in New York City and their home on Riverside Drive. He wrote *Adventure Capitalist* following this around-the-world adventure. It is currently one of his bestselling books.

https://en.wikipedia.org/wiki/Jim_Rogers

78. **Robert Shiller:** Born March 29, 1946, is an American economist (Nobel Laureate in 2013), academic, and best-selling author. As of 2018, he serves as a Sterling Professor of Economics at Yale University and is a fellow at the Yale School of Management's International Center for Finance.

https://en.wikipedia.org/wiki/Robert_J._Shiller

79. **Marc Faber:** Born February 28, 1946, is a Swiss investor based in Thailand. Faber is publisher of the *Gloom Boom & Doom Report* newsletter and is the director of Marc Faber Ltd, which acts as an investment advisor and fund manager.

https://en.wikipedia.org/wiki/Marc_Faber

80. **Steve Forbes Jr.:** Born July 18, 1947, is an American publishing executive, who was twice a candidate for the nomination of the Republican Party for President of the United States. Forbes is the Editor-in-Chief of *Forbes*, a business magazine.

https://en.wikipedia.org/wiki/Steve_Forbes

81. **Peter David Schiff:** Born March 23, 1963, is an American stock broker, financial commentator, and radio personality. He is CEO and chief global strategist of Euro Pacific Capital Inc., a broker-dealer based in Westport, Connecticut.

https://en.wikipedia.org/wiki/Peter_Schiff

82. **Dan Gainor:** Is the Vice President of Business and Culture for the MRC and has been with the organization for more than 10 years. He heads up both our MRC Business and MRC Culture departments, including our popular Soros Project. He is a veteran editor with more than three decades of experience in print and online media. Gainor has appeared on Fox News, the Fox Business Network, CNN, CNN HN, CBS, NBC, CNBC, EWTN, The Blaze, and

Newsmax TV and has a regular spot on the One America News Network.

https://www.mrc.org/staff/dan-gainor

83. **George Franklin Gilder:** Born November 29, 1939, is an American investor, writer, economist, techno-utopian advocate, and co-founder of the Discovery Institute.

https://en.wikipedia.org/wiki/George_Gilder

84. **Amazon.com, Inc.:** Is an American multinational technology company based in Seattle, Washington that focuses in e-commerce, cloud computing, and artificial intelligence.

Amazon is the largest e-commerce marketplace and cloud computing platform in the world as measured by revenue and market capitalization. Amazon.com was founded by Jeff Bezos on July 5, 1994 and started as an online bookstore but later diversified to sell video downloads/streaming.

https://en.wikipedia.org/wiki/Amazon_(company)

85. **Apple Inc.:** Is an American multinational technology company headquartered in Cupertino, California, that designs, develops, and sells consumer electronics, computer software, and online services. It is considered one of the Big Four of technology along with Amazon, Google, and Facebook. The company's hardware products include the iPhone smartphone, the iPad tablet computer, the Mac personal computer, the iPod portable media player, the Apple Watch smartwatch, the Apple TV digital media player, and the HomePod smart speaker.

https://en.wikipedia.org/wiki/Apple_Inc.

86. **NetFlix, Inc.:** Is an American media-services provider headquartered in Los Gatos, California, founded in 1997 by Reed Hastings and Marc Randolph in Scotts Valley, California. The company's primary business is its subscription-based streaming OTT service which offers online streaming of a library of films and television programs, including those produced in-house.

https://en.wikipedia.org/wiki/Netflix

87. **Enron Corporation:** Was an American energy, commodities, and services company based in Houston, Texas. It was founded in 1985 as a merger between Houston Natural Gas and InterNorth, both

relatively small regional companies. Before its bankruptcy on December 3, 2001, Enron employed approximately 29,000 staff and was a major electricity, natural gas, communications and pulp and paper company, with claimed revenues of nearly $101 billion during 2000. *Fortune* named Enron "America's Most Innovative Company" for six consecutive years.

https://en.wikipedia.org/wiki/Enron

88. **WorldCom:** The WorldCom bankruptcy proceedings were held before U.S. Federal Bankruptcy Judge Arthur J. Gonzalez, who simultaneously heard the Enron bankruptcy proceedings, which were the second largest bankruptcy case resulting from one of the largest corporate fraud scandals. None of the criminal proceedings against WorldCom and its officers and agents were originated by referral from Gonzalez or the Department of Justice lawyers. By the bankruptcy reorganization agreement, the company paid $750 million to the SEC in cash and stock in the new MCI, which was intended to be paid to wronged investors.

https://en.wikipedia.org/wiki/MCI_Inc.

CHARTS

4 Source Chart A—Standard and Poor's 500—Thirteen Years of No Growth:

https://finance.yahoo.com/quote/%5EGSPC?p=^GSPC

2000—The Bubble Bursts: At the turn of the century, the S&P 500 would crack 1,500 for the first time, before embarking on a three-year slide that began with the bursting of the internet bubble and losses of 9% for the index for the year as a whole.

https://etfdb.com/history-of-the-s-and-p-500/#2000

2008—The Great Recession:

No major shifts as far as the top 10 are concerned, but 2008 is a year many investors remember well, as the S&P 500 took a nasty tumble. The bellwether index lost more than 36%, as the U.S. financial crisis wreaked havoc on equities across the board. This would, unfortunately, only be the beginning of global economic woes, which spread to other areas of the world in the coming months and years.

https://etfdb.com/history-of-the-s-and-p-500/#2008

7 Source Chart B—World Life Expectancy Since 1770:

Life expectancy (James Riley for data 1990 and earlier; WHO and World Bank for later data [by Max Roser]).

"Development Review." *Population and Development Review.* Volume 31, Issue 3, pages 537–543, September 2005.

http://onlinelibrary.wiley.com/ doi/10.1111/j.1728-4457.2005.00083.x/epdf

11 Source Chart C—Dow Jones Industrial Average—1982 to 2000:

Data is available from July 2, 1982 DJIA of 797.00 points to DJIA January 3, 2000 of 11,522.56 points and suggests a growth of about 14 times. From Data supplied by Samuel H. Williamson, 'Daily Closing Value of the Dow Jones Average, 1885 to Present,' MeasuringWorth, 2015.

https://finance.yahoo.com/quote/%5EDJI/history?ltr=1

61 Source Chart D—S&P 500 Secular Bear Market—1966 to 1982:

Data is available from January 1, 1966 S&P 500 of 93.32 points to S&P 500 December 1, 1982 of 139.40 points. Showing Bull and Bear Markets.

https://finance.yahoo.com/quote/%5EGSPC/history?ltr=1

65 Source Chart E—Dow Jones Industrial Average—1929 to 1954:

From Data supplied by Samuel H. Williamson, 'Daily Closing Value of the Dow Jones Average, 1885 to Present,' MeasuringWorth, 2015.

https://finance.yahoo.com/quote/%5EDJI/history?ltr=1

66 Source Chart F—S&P 500 Secular Bear Market—1966 to 1982:

Data is available from January 1, 1966 S&P 500 of 93.32 points to S&P 500 December 1, 1982 of 139.40 points.

https://finance.yahoo.com/quote/%5EGSPC/history?ltr=1

69 Source Chart G—S&P 500 Composite Index—1900 to 2019:

The S&P 500, or just the S&P, is an American stock market index based on the market capitalizations of 500 large companies having common stock listed on the NYSE, NASDAQ, or the Cboe BZX Exchange.

https://en.wikipedia.org/wiki/S%26P_500_Index

https://finance.yahoo.com/quote/%5EGSPC/history?p=%5EGSPC

71 Source Chart H—Price of S&P 500 Profits Calculated as Average of Previous 10 Years:

Price earnings ratio is based on average inflation-adjusted earnings from the previous 10 years, known as the Cyclically -Adjusted PE Ratio, data courtesy of Robert Shiller.

https://www.multpl.com/shiller-pe

73 Source Chart I—U.S. 10-Year Treasury Bond Rate 1954 to 2019:

As Robert Shiller's new 2009 preface to his prescient classic on behavioral economics and market volatility asserts, the irrational exuberance of the stock and housing markets "has been ended by an economic crisis of a magnitude not seen since the Great Depression of the 1930s."

- US Treasury for recent 10 Year Treasury Rates.
- Robert Shiller and his book *Irrational Exuberance* for long-term historic 10 Year Treasury Yields.

https://www.multpl.com/10-year-treasury-rate

80 Source Chart J—Federal Reserve Balance Sheet 2007 to 2019:

Since the beginning of the financial market turmoil in August 2007, the Federal Reserve's balance sheet has grown in size and has changed in composition. Total assets of the Federal Reserve have increased significantly from $870 billion on August 8, 2007, to 4.5 trillion on January 14, 2015, and have been declining since the beginning of the FOMC's balance sheet normalization program in October 2017.

https://www.federalreserve.gov/monetarypolicy/bst_recenttrends.htm

83 Source Chart K—FINRA Margin Debt—1997 to 2019:

Margin Debt Pursuant to FINRA Rule 4521, FINRA member firms carrying margin accounts for customers are required to submit, on a settlement date basis, as of the last business day of the month, the following customer information:

- The total of all debit balances in securities margin accounts; and
- The total of all free credit balances in all cash accounts and all securities margin accounts.

Debit Balances are derived by adding NYSE Debit Balances in Margin Accounts to FINRA Debit Balances in Customers' Cash and Margin Accounts.

http://www.finra.org/investors/margin-statistics

84 Source Chart L—FINRA Margin Debt—1997 to 2019:

Margin Statistics Pursuant to FINRA Rule 4521, FINRA member firms carrying margin accounts for customers are required to submit, on a settlement date basis, as of the last business day of the month, the following customer information:

- The total of all debit balances in securities margin accounts; and
- The total of all free credit balances in all cash accounts and all securities margin accounts.

FINRA collects the required data via FINRA's Customer Margin Balance Form. The data is compiled in aggregate form and made available below. See Regulatory Notice 10-08 (Customer Margin Accounts) for more information.

http://www.finra.org/investors/margin-statistics

85 Source Chart M—S&P 500 Share Buybacks:

The amount of shares repurchased by S&P 500 companies in the last three months of 2018 hit a record, marking the fourth consecutive quarterly all-time high and the longest such streak since S&P Dow Jones Indices began tracking repurchases two decades ago. Source: FactSet Fundamentals. https://www.marketwatch.com/story/stock-buybacks-among-sp-500-companies-mark-a-record-streak-2019-03-25

SOURCE DATA:

https://www.google.com/search?rlz=1C1CHBF_
enUS801US801&biw=1920&bih=920&tbm=isch&sa=1&ei=
Dq_IXIyI4zisAXlzob4Bg&q=s%26p+500+share+buybacks++
factset+fundamentals&oq=s%26p+500+share+buybacks++
factset+fundamentals&gs_l=img.3...68939.68939..69182...0.0..0.
114.114.0j1......0....1..gws-wiz-img.3Q0eOHUxqy4#imgrc=
6r7_mqZvlmckLM:

88 Source Chart N—Dow Jones Industrial Average—Bulls & Bears—1966 to 1982:

Citation Samuel H. Williamson, Daily Closing Value of the Dow Jones Average, 1885 to Present, MeasuringWorth.

https://finance.yahoo.com/quote/%5EDJI/history?ltr=1

143 Source Chart O—World GDP Per Capita in 1990 Dollars:

Year 1-2008 AD (Copyright Angus Maddison).

http://www.ggdc.net/maddison/oriindex.htm

http://worldpopulationreview.com/countries/countries-by-gdp/

https://www.focus-economics.com/blog/the-largest-economies-in-the-world

http://www.worldbank.org/en/publication/global-economic-prospects

http://www.economywatch.com/economic-statistics/year/2019/

146 Source Chart P—S&P 500 Composite Index:

The S&P 500, or just the S&P, is an American stock market index based on the market capitalizations of 500 large companies having common stock listed on the NYSE, NASDAQ, or the Cboe BZX Exchange.

https://en.wikipedia.org/wiki/S%26P_500_Index

https://finance.yahoo.com/quote/%5EGSPC/history?p=%5EGSPC

148 Source Chart Q—Federal Debt: Total Public Debt as Percent of Gross Domestic Product

Was first constructed by the Federal Reserve Bank of St. Louis in October 2012. It is calculated using Federal Government Debt: Total Public Debt (GFDEBTN) and Gross Domestic Product, 1 Decimal (GDP): GFDEGDQ188S = ((GFDEBTN/1000)/GDP)*100 GFDEBTN/1000 transforms GFDEBTN from millions of dollars to billions of dollars. Suggested Citation: Federal Reserve Bank of St. Louis and U.S. Office of Management and Budget, Federal Debt: Total Public Debt as Percent of Gross Domestic Product [GFDEGDQ188S], retrieved from FRED, Federal Reserve Bank of St. Louis; https://fred.stlouisfed.org/series/GFDEGDQ188S, April 24, 2019.

https://fred.stlouisfed.org/series/GFDEGDQ188S#0

159 Source Chart R—Millennials, Gen X and Boomers - Transamerica Center for Retirement Studies:

Retirement Studies about the saving habits of three generations of Americans, they all share similar views about how to save for and enjoy their future retirement.

http://money.com/money/5640466/this-chart-shows-how-much-millennials-gen-x-and-baby-boomers-have-saved-for-retirement-see-how-you-compare/

TABLES

https://www.jstor.org/stable/23700715?seq=1#page_scan_tab_contents

The Hard Lessons of Stock Market History:

http://www.summitgp.com/wp-content/uploads/2018/01/Caicedo.Hard-Lessons-of-Stock-Market-History.01.08.18.pdf

1928-1954 Stock Chart Pre-Through-Post Great Depression Era:

You can see by looking at this 1928-1954 stock chart, that once the bottom was finally in place in late 1932, the market gradually rose over the next two decades. Notice that it took just about 25 years from the peak in the stock market in 1929 for it to reach this level again.

http://www.online-stock-trading-guide.com/1928-1954-stock-chart.html

Eleven Historic Bear Markets:

By one common definition, a bear market occurs when stock prices fall for a sustained period, dropping at least 20 percent from their peak. The Great Recession was accompanied by a painful bear market that lasted nearly a year and a half.

Here is a look at some notable bear markets of the past 80 years, with the crash of 1929 shown for comparison.

http://www.nbcnews.com/id/37740147/ns/business-stocks_and_economy/t/historic-bear-markets/#.XMsYWNh7lD0

Bond mutual funds are mutual funds that invest in bonds. Like other mutual funds, bond mutual funds are like baskets that hold dozens or hundreds of individual securities (in this case, bonds). A bond fund manager or team of managers will research the fixed income markets for the best bonds based upon the overall objective of the bond mutual fund. The manager(s) will then purchase and sell bonds based upon economic and market activity. Managers also have to sell funds to meet redemptions (withdrawals) of investors.

https://www.thebalance.com/bonds-vs-bond-funds-2466790

Individual Bonds—A Higher Probability That You Receive Your Principal Back:

One allure of fixed income investing is that in the case of most individual bonds, investors can be assured that they will receive their principal back upon the bond's maturity. While only bonds backed by the U.S. government - U.S. Treasuries and other bonds backed by the U.S. government, such as savings bonds - even higher-risk market segments feature low historical rates of default (failure to make interest or principal payments) among individual securities. This is particularly true among issues with the highest credit ratings.

https://www.thebalance.com/individual-bonds-vs-bond-funds-416972

INDEX

Note: Page numbers in italics indicate figures; page numbers followed by "t" indicate tables.